As this book was going to press, we learned of the passing of James Garner, July 19, 2014, at his home in Brentwood, California. Mr. Garner, 86, is survived by his wife Lois, two daughters, and many great acting roles, characters, and his love of cars and motorsport.

JAMES GARNER'S
Motoring Life

Grand Prix the Movie, Baja, *The Rockford Files*, and More

MATT STONE

Foreword by Bob Bondurant

CarTech®

CarTech®, Inc.
39966 Grand Avenue
North Branch, MN 55056
Phone: 651-277-1200 or 800-551-4754
Fax: 651-277-1203
www.cartechbooks.com

Edit by Bob Wilson and Wes Eisenschenk
Layout by Chris Fayers

ISBN 978-1-61325-136-2
Item No. CT529

Library of Congress Cataloging-in-Publication Data

Stone, Matt
 James Garner's motoring life / by Matt Stone.
   pages cm
 Includes index.
 ISBN 978-1-61325-136-2
1. Garner, James. 2. Automobile racing drivers--United States--Biography. 3. Motion picture actors and actresses--United States--Biography. I. Title.

GV1032.G385S86 2014
796.72092--dc23
[B]
                    2014007008

Written, edited, and designed in the U.S.A.
Printed in China
10 9 8 7 6 5 4 3 2 1

Front Cover: Regardless of whether he's in character as *Grand Prix*'s Pete Aron or as himself, the actor, car enthusiast, racer, and sports car racing team owner has a look that is unmistakably James Garner: lanky 6-foot 3-inch frame, classically chiseled face, wavy dark hair, and beaming from-the-heart smile. Here, Garner, as Aron, stands atop a winner's podium during the filming of *Grand Prix*. At this stage in his life, during the mid-1960s and not yet 40 years old, Garner could have made a credible career for himself as a professional racing driver had he chosen that path. *Photo Courtesy Everett Collection*

Front Flap: "The "I" in A.I.R. is particularly prominent in this logo, as if to differentiate James Garner's racing team from Dan Gurney's All American Racers (AAR). *Photo Courtesy Richard Prince*

End Papers: On the left is Eric Dahlquist, Sr., former editor of *Hot Rod* and *Motor Trend* magazines, and longtime public relations and product placement executive and principal of Vista Group. At right of course is James Garner. The interesting car in the foreground is a General Motors Design Study based on the new-for 1979 Pontiac Firebird styling, loosely referred to as the Kammback Trans Am. The Rockford-spec Firebird at rear is likely a 1978; it was the car still in use in the production when the 1979 concept car was built. *Photo Courtesy Vista Group*

Frontispiece: Bob Bondurant rides shotgun in a Shelby GT350 as a grinning James Garner drives. James Garner enjoyed driving and racing from the word "go" and had the attitude and mentality of a professional racing driver. *Photo Courtesy Bondurant School*

Title Page: James Garner as Pete Aron leads a pack of Formula One machines through Monza's storied high-bank turns. *Photo Courtesy MGM/Getty Images*

Table of Contents: Lots of customer interaction and promotional activity was an important part of the A.I.R business plan. Here all the A.I.R. team cars make a visit to Southern California Clippinger Chevrolet for a promotional event and traffic draw for the dealership. *Photo Courtesy Davey Jordan Collection*

Back Cover Photos

Top: The seminal Jim Rockford look, circa season one, 1974. James Garner never was more handsome with the trademark shades, long-sleeved dress shirt, soda cup from a fast-food joint, and a gold 1974 Firebird. *Photo Courtesy H.L./mptvimages.com*

Middle: This high-angle view gives a better look at how much shorter and squatter the *Banshee* is than a conventional, production-bodied 1969 4-4-2, and that the original body-colored steel wheels have given way to more modern alloy wheels. *Photo Courtesy Mel Stone*

Bottom: Handsome and elegant Japanese actor Toshiro Mifune portrays industrialist and racing team owner/car builder Izo Yamura. It is said that this name was made up as a spin on the Japanese industrial firm Yamaha. Mr. Yamura gives Pete Aron a break when his luck is really down, and invites him to the Yamura shop to be fitted for his new race car. *Photo Courtesy Camerique/Getty Images*

OVERSEAS DISTRIBUTION BY:

PGUK
63 Hatton Garden
London EC1N 8LE, England
Phone: 020 7061 1980 • Fax: 020 7242 3725
www.pguk.co.uk

Renniks Publications Ltd.
3/37-39 Green Street
Banksmeadow, NSW 2109, Australia
Phone: 2 9695 7055 • Fax: 2 9695 7355
www.renniks.com

CONTENTS

ACKNOWLEDGMENTS

and My Thanks . . .

Pat and Bob Bondurant, Eric Dahlquist, everyone at CarTech Books, Slick Gardner, Evi and Dan Gurney, Chuck Koch, John Kyros, Norma and Davey Jordan, Parnelli Jones, Lori Lovely, Tom Madigan, John and Vickie Mendenhall, Jim Ober, Scooter Patrick, Fred Phillips, Richard Prince, John Prumatico, Steve Reich, Pat McKinney, MPTVImages.com, Ralph Todd, Richard Truesdell, Linda Stone, Mel Stone, Willie Stroppe, Jim Suva, Jon Swift, Bill Warner, Kathy Wieda, Jon Winokur, and anyone else that helped me along the way, named or accidentally unnamed.

And, of course, the incomparable James Garner.

FOREWORD

by Bob Bondurant

Bob Bondurant is a multi-talented American racing driver; Grand Prix director John Frankenheimer engaged him as a racing consultant and actor/driver coach for the production. Bondurant, born in Evanston, Illinois, in 1933, began his racing career running dirt-track motorcycles in the Midwest before switching to road racing vehicles with four wheels; "Bondo" was a successful pro-level road racer beginning in the early 1960s until a Can-Am racing accident brought about his retirement in 1967. He was more than qualified for the task director Frankenheimer had in mind. Bondurant contested a total of nine Grands Prix during his Formula One career in 1965 and 1966; he drove for the Ferrari North American Racing Team, Dan Gurney's All American Racers, and others.

Bondurant is a natural teacher, with a friendly, disarming, yet authoritative style that encourages students rather than intimating them. He had also dreamed of opening a high-performance driving and racing school long before his accident and retirement. He was tailor-made for the job of getting the Grand Prix acting team "up to speed."

I've known James Garner for nearly 50 years. He's a real man, fantastic actor, very handsome, and very married. Jim was great to work with and a great friend. I really got to know him when I trained him for John Frankenheimer's movie *Grand Prix*. He definitely enjoyed the movie *Grand Prix* and real Grand Prix racing.

He liked everyone and they enjoyed and respected him. As a happily married man he never looked at or flirted with other ladies. Director Frankenheimer felt Jim's character, as an American, should be driving a black and gold Shelby Mustang GT-350H at different times in the film. However, he didn't really like to drive on the street in Europe, so he let me drive it. I have to tell

Bob Bondurant's ERA GT40 Mk I tribute car was built using a variety of authentic period GT40 parts; "Bondo" brought the car to Auto Club Speedway in Fontana, California, serving as pace car and driver for a recent Shelby and Cobra club meet and vintage race. Although Bondurant raced a variety of cars during his legendary career, and currently populates his driving school fleet with Chevrolets, it's hard to think of him as anything other than a Ford and Shelby guy.

"Legends, Heros, and Friends" might as well be the title of this historic photo, from a racer's night gala at the Petersen Automotive Museum in Los Angeles. From left, America's first F1 champ, the late Phil Hill; the All American Racer Dan Gurney; the late Carroll Shelby; Bob Bondurant; Indy 500, Trans-Am champ and Baja legend Parnelli Jones; and road racer extraordinaire John Morton.

you, it was a fantastic hot car in Europe, especially around Monaco, and it was the only one in all of Europe. It was like driving a Ferrari over here. Garner's stand-in and I both loved the car and I drove it around the circuits when we weren't filming.

Jim Russell's instructors trained the other actors. Just before we landed at London's Heathrow Airport, John Frankenheimer said to me, "Bob you are now responsible for training the other actors: Brian Bedford, Yves Montand, and Antonio Sabato." Jim Russell didn't like it at all, so we worked it out so that his instructors would train them [the basics] and I was to work with them to get them up to speed. They were being trained in Formula Fords only. Yves Montand did well, but the other actors had never driven a car before, but they all ultimately got better. James Garner did a fantastic job, and all four of the actors got along great.

Every circuit we raced was a real Formula One circuit. American Phil Hill and I were hired as technical advisors and we toured all of the circuits. Phil helped write the script since he had raced for Ferrari for many years and in 1961 was the first American to win the Formula One title.

James Garner did a great job in Monaco and at all the big circuits throughout Europe. Coincidentally, when Frankenheimer shot *Grand Prix*, Formula One's governing body, the Federation Internationale de l'Automobile (FIA) changed the engine size from 1.5 liters to 3.0 liters. The teams sold their outdated cars to Frankenheimer, with the exception

James Garner and Bob Bondurant at Willow Springs Raceway in California, in 1964 during driver training for the upcoming filming of *Grand Prix*. I'm not sure why the intent stares, but teacher and student alike appear to be concentrating very hard on something. Check out those split-lens goggles. *Photo Courtesy Bondurant School*

of Enzo Ferrari, who would not sell. All the actors were able to learn how to race in a real Formula One car. I brought them up to speed and they ultimately did well.

When I trained Garner in Formula Fords and a real Formula One car, he did fantastic and loved racing. He had such great natural talent, listened, and learned well. It is quite possible that if he'd started out much younger, and came up through the ranks the way Phil Hill, Dan Gurney, Masten Gregory, and I did, he might have enjoyed a good career as a professional racer. After filming the movie, Jim went on to off-road racing and did very well; he even launched and ran his own professional racing team for a few years. In this book, author Matt Stone tells James Garner's story as racing actor, race team owner, and car guy. I bet you'll learn some things about him that you didn't know and enjoy some never-before-seen photos. Four decades ago, when I opened my high-performance driving school, James Garner and Datsun's legendary "Mr. K" were there with me; Jim and I are still great friends.

That's always James Garner: loyal, a class act, and a great car guy.

Bob Bondurant

A trio of Clark Gable's great cars visit the Petersen Automotive Museum in Los Angeles: his mildly customized 1941 Cadillac (left), his "Gable Gray" 1949 Jaguar XK-120 (center), along with the rare and fabulous 1956 Mercedes-Benz 300 Sc Cabriolet (right) that he still owned at the time of his passing. More proof that great stars love great cars.

Hollywood has always had its great car guys. It only makes sense: Hollywood actors, producers, directors, agents, and other entertainment industry heavies wield a combination of money, power, and fame. Most of the time, they could have what they wanted: a high-visibility role, a star-worthy home, women who appealed to them, and the latest greatest cars.

Clark Gable was always serious about his cars. Cadillac, Duesenberg, Jaguar, Mercedes-Benz; he had them all, and more often than not he was involved in their design and specification. Great cars were more than show ponies to him; there's little question that The Great Gable *got* it.

The late 1950s and 1960s gave us (at least) one holy trinity of great Hollywood car guys. Consider Steve McQueen, Paul Newman, and James Garner. To an only somewhat lesser extent, add James Coburn, Clint Eastwood, Peter Sellers, and others to that august list.

The man we know and love as James Garner was born James Scott Bumgarner on April 7, 1928, in the humble southern burb of Norman, Oklahoma. One of three brothers, he lived a modest yet occasionally complicated young life, served his country in the American Armed Forces, and was honorably discharged. He even did a little modeling before his acting career really got traction.

Somehow you can tell from the look on director John Sturges' face (wearing hat, at right) that there's likely mischief afoot with three of his cheerful lead actors on the set of *The Great Escape*. The shirtless McQueen was likely the instigator, with Garner riding behind him, and a young James Coburn reclining in the sidecar. All were friends and West Los Angeles–area neighbors. *Photo Courtesy UA/Photofest*

James Garner is also one serious and committed car guy; which of course is why I've written this book.

He tells his story with great humility, clarity, and passion in his autobiography, *The Garner Files*, co-written with Jon Winokur, first published in 2012; I refer to it often. In it you learn much that you likely didn't know about this self-deprecating, humble, frequently shy acting hero. He's acted on stage and is one of the few actors to make an entirely successful transition from the small screen to the big screen (in both directions, often simultaneously). He already had many successful movie roles to his credit when he reinvented the notion of a likeable, charming, small-time California private investigator to portray Jim Rockford in *The Rockford Files*, which first aired as a prime time weekly series in 1974. Mr. Garner's autobiography lists his complete filmography, so I won't recount it here. He's also well known and liked for television commercials, long before bragging rights over memorable Super Bowl commercials came to light.

James Garner is also one serious and committed car guy; which of course is why I've written this book. You won't read about what kind of cereal he eats for breakfast or the "tell all" tales of girlfriends prior to his marriage to his only wife Lois. Something else you may not know about James Garner is that he participated in the famous "March on Washington for Jobs and Freedom" in August 1963. In addition, he stood a mere few feet from Dr. Martin Luther King, Jr., as he gave the famous "I Have a Dream" speech. Otherwise, if you're interested in paparazzi stuff about James Garner, shop elsewhere (and good luck finding any).

He's owned and driven some nice street cars along the way. It seems that his enthusiasm for cars really lit up during his training for, and the filming of, his fabulous movie about the danger, drama, beauty, and glory of Formula One racing, *Grand Prix*. It was directed by John Frankenheimer and released to wide critical acclaim in 1966. Garner gave a fine and solid acting performance, and trained hard to look, act, and drive like a real Formula One racing driver. He did his own high-speed driving in the film, which I will talk a lot about, and was absolutely credible in doing so.

During his storied life, as well as his movie and television career, Steve McQueen had to choose between acting and racing several times, often at the behest of his agents and studio chiefs. Only upon becoming a studio principal of his own company, Solar Productions, was he able to consistently drive his own stunts and participate in motorsports. By the time Paul Newman actively pursued a career in racing and as a race team owner, he was so wealthy, influential, and in demand that he just did as he wished, and the studios loved, hated, or otherwise endured it. James Garner actively escalated his participation as a racing driver after the making of *Grand Prix*, and somehow walked the line between acting, television production company boss, and motorsport; he appeared to be able to keep them all balanced with little interference from one another.

In the late 1960s, James Garner, like Steve McQueen, discovered the joys and challenges of off-road desert racing. Garner, in partnership with four other principals, also launched a successful pro-level road racing team, American International Racing (A.I.R., not to be confused with Dan Gurney's All American Racers, AAR). During the team's short three-year life, Garner raced less and less as a driver, and grew more comfortable in the role of team owner and car builder. All that changed when Garner was starring in *The Rockford Files*, with the actor capably doing virtually all of his own action and some stunt driving at the wheel of a rumbling gold Pontiac Firebird.

I met James Garner only once; it was at a motoring press trade association dinner that hosted a *Grand Prix* panel. Bob Bondurant, *Grand Prix*'s ace second unit action camera man John M. Stephens, America's first Formula One champion Phil Hill, and James Garner sat on that panel. In person, Garner seemed an easy-going amalgam of every character I loved watching him portray: Jim Rockford, Pete Aron, Bart Maverick, and Murphy Jones from his Academy Award–nominated performance in *Murphy's Romance.* He was well into his seventies at the time, still tall and handsome, with a deep, rich voice and a comfortable, "old Hollywood" gravitas that radiated from him effortlessly. He told stories about the making of the film with obvious enthusiasm, and couldn't have been more cordial, staying long after the program was over, casually chatting with anyone who approached him, including me. I won't forget that night. Ever.

I'll talk about the street cars he owned and drove, cars he raced, the drama and dust of pounding through the desolate Baja Peninsula, his tour of duty as a racing team owner, his Great Racing Film, and his commanding ability as a television action driver. Please enjoy the ride as you follow some of the footsteps taken by James Garner, racing actor, racing team owner, and automotive enthusiast.

Garner, with co-author Jon Winokur, tells his story well, with honesty, humor, and grace, in his long-awaited autobiography, *The Garner Files*. In it you learn about his youth, family, politics, racing, acting, producing, many great co-stars and friends, plus his entire filmography and television history. Every James Garner fan needs a copy of this *New York Times* Best Seller List book.

THE
GARNER FILES
A MEMOIR

"You could hand this book as a primer on ethics to any young man just reaching the age of choosing his way in life."
—CLIVE JAMES,
THE ATLANTIC

JAMES GARNER
AND JON WINOKUR
INTRODUCTION BY JULIE ANDREWS

GARNER'S GARAGE *A Few Favorites*

A well-dressed James Garner speaks about his beloved Mini; he is quoted as saying this is one of his all-time favorite cars. James Garner and Steve McQueen were by no means the only entertainers to enjoy Mini motoring; several members of the Beatles owned them, Peter Sellers had a pair that were heavily customized. And who could forget its important role in the great chase flicks, the original *The Italian Job* and the recent remake. *Photo © 1978 Gunther, via mptvimages.com*

" When I took my wife, Lois, to the premiere of *West Side Story*, I was so ashamed of my old heap, I had to borrow Natalie Wood's Cadillac

— *James Garner* "

In an interview published in *Car and Driver* magazine's May 2012 issue, James Garner spoke about some of his earliest automotive experiences, noting that his first car was a gray 1952 Dodge coupe. "It wasn't quite a 'rolling disaster,' but it was ugly. I bought it with my mustering-out pay from the army, plus the cash I won in a poker game on the ship home from Korea.

Chapter One

"Cars were a luxury *and* a necessity when I started driving at the age of 10. They were a luxury because we were poor. They were a necessity because we loved them. By the time I was 13 or 14, I was playing 'ditch 'em.' We'd line up six or eight cars, and the first one would take off and try to lose the rest. Or, if I was cruising around town and I saw another hotshot, I'd get behind him and tap his bumper, and the race would be on.

"It was during World War II, and gas was rationed, so we had to steal it. We'd go up to a car in the middle of the night and siphon off a few gallons. We had fun, and nobody got hurt because we were all good drivers. At least we thought we were. Maybe we were just lucky."

A Few Old Favorites

One car Garner may wish he had today is his 1956 Plymouth Fury hardtop. Automotive author, broadcaster, and muscle-car expert Steve Magnante had this to say about it: "A very cool machine, the 1956 Plymouth Fury. It was Plymouth's first 'muscle car' and approximately 4,500 were built. All were cream and gold two-door hardtops. No lame four-doors or wagons. Engines were nothing less than the 303-ci polyspherical-head V-8 with 240 hp, single 4-barrel carburetor, and dual exhaust. The dual-quads [and fins] didn't arrive until 1957."

It looks like beach day for the Garner family, as daughter Kimberly, father James, and mom Lois Garner load up their rare 1956 Plymouth Fury "family muscle car." *Photo Courtesy Everett Collection*

"

Gene told me that one night he spotted a dark navy blue 1949–1951 Mercury coupe, and 'driving it was about the handsomest guy I'd ever seen.'

"

My friend the late Gene Garfinkle relayed to me one particularly interesting James Garner–and-car sighting from the mid-1950s after Garner landed in Los Angeles. Garfinkle was an independent automotive and industrial designer, ex–General Motors, who frequented the Saturday cruise nights at Bob's Big Boy Restaurant in Burbank, California. Gene told me that one night he spotted a dark navy blue 1949–1951 Mercury coupe, and "driving it was about the handsomest guy I'd ever seen." Of course it was a young James Garner, by himself, cruising the lot looking for a spot to park and order a burger. Garfinkle recalls approaching to compliment the driver about his car, and that "Garner was very friendly, happy to talk and chat about the car."

Television and movie studios have long used automobiles as gifts (or bait) with their bigger-name stars, either to encourage them to sign onto a project, reward or acknowledge their role in a particularly successful one, or apologize for a situation that went bad. James Garner got a taste of the latter in the late 1950s, over a terms-and-contract dispute with his studio involving an appearance on *The Pat Boone Chevy Showroom* show on ABC, which the studio execs expected him to make at no charge. In *The Garner Files*, he describes the discussion getting as far as threats to fire him and of lawsuits. After all was said and done, Garner was paid $2,500 for his appearance on the Boone show, and given a new 1959 Corvette, tax-free. He commented that he "wishes he had that car today!" It was black, and as with any car he owned or drove, always immaculate.

James Garner in the mid-1950s with two of his passions represented in this photo: golf and cars. The 1956 Fury just behind was a special and rare car when new, and remains so today. A cousin of sorts to the vaunted Chrysler 300 of the mid-1950s, they were at first sold only in crème white paint with gold trim. *Photo Courtesy Sid Avery/mptvimages.com*

According to friends and other anecdotal sources, the Garner's West Los Angeles–area driveway was a relatively busy place. There were several Mustangs and Jaguars, and at least one Ferrari.

In the opening frame of *The Racing Scene* documentary (filmed in 1969; more later) Garner is at the wheel of a light yellow 1968 or 1969 Corvette 427 coupe, although it is not clear if he owned the car or if it was provided by Chevrolet for promotional purposes. Several other current-model Chevrolets are seen in the film, and many Chevrolets were also used later in the filming of *The Rockford Files*.

Clowning for the camera in, and just out of, his Mini sometime in 1966. The original Mini was a masterwork of clever packaging, obviously able to accommodate tall passengers front and back, as well as a modicum of luggage in the boot. *Photo © 1978 Gunther, via mptvimages.com*

A Couple Minis

To date, James Garner has owned two Minis. One was an early- to mid-1960s dark blue Mini Cooper with which he was often photographed, and the other was a later (also blue) BMW-generation Mini Cooper. The original Mini is known as a marvel of automotive packaging, able to squeeze four adults and a modicum of luggage or cargo into its compact, friendly boxlike shape. That was important for James Garner, who in his prime stood about 6 feet 3 inches. He only needed to sit up a little straighter than usual and open the large Webasto sunroof wide to drive with his head completely outside the passenger compartment; something he likely didn't do often.

Garner lived a mostly friendly, if occasionally competitive, existence with his Brentwood, California, neighbor Steve McQueen. Both were highly competitive, top-rung stars who, once in a while, vied for the same roles; and each dabbled seriously with cars and motorsport. Their kids grew up together, their wives are friends, and they visited each other's homes for the occasional barbecue or party. McQueen, who owned a fabulous fleet of cars and bikes, also drove a Mini Cooper for a time in the 1960s. Is it any wonder, then, that the pair staged their own "Brentwood Grand Prix," racing each other in their Minis, up and down the hilly residential streets in their neighborhood? Who won most often? Who knows?

Opposite: One of James Garner's American International Racing Lolas at Sebring, 1969. The perfect thing for cruising up and down Sunset Boulevard near his West Los Angeles home? *Photo Courtesy Bill Warner*

Garner with his *James Garner Special*. This is not your average street car, nor your average race car; it has room for several passengers. The wings and aero aids look functional if unconventional; one can only imagine that the car never underwent any meaningful aerodynamics testing. It is reported that passengers in the outboard seats got a face full of sand and grit, despite the windscreen and the deep-set cockpit. This photo was taken at what was then called Sears Point Raceway in Sonoma, California. *Photo Courtesy Davey Jordan Collection*

In 2011, in the British newspaper *Express*, Garner is quoted, saying of McQueen: "He wasn't a bad guy, just insecure. But deep down, he thought of me as an older brother and I guess I thought of him as a delinquent younger brother."

Lola Coupes

James Garner's pro-level road racing team, A.I.R., competed in several series with a variety of vehicles, including cars built for big-time professional endurance racing. Among the team's weapons of choice were Chevrolet V-8–powered British Lola T70 coupes. This model Lola is a beautiful machine, and although it is hardly a typical street car, being equipped for endurance road racing meant that the car had to have headlights, taillights, and brake lights.

During the late 1960s and early 1970s, it wasn't uncommon for these machines to be converted for street use, or simply driven on the street in full race trim. In 1969, James Garner did exactly that: "The Lolas were sweet. *Great* race cars. What I wouldn't give to have one now. I drove one on the street for quite a while, but the lights were too low. Totally against the law."

Ralph Todd is a South African transplant who, at the time, worked for England's Lola Cars. One of his tasks while stationed in the United States was to provide a certain amount of support to teams running Lolas in North American competition. Todd is a certified engineer, and lives and breathes motor racing, so he was well qualified for the job.

Todd recalls one day when his "phone rang, and the caller was a friendly, but somewhat agitated-sounding fellow who introduced himself as 'Jim Garner.' Mr. Garner noted that he'd spun his Lola T70 on the street and 'knocked off a few corners,'" In other words, he'd damaged a combination of wheels and suspension components.

"He asked if I could supply the parts to repair his car. Unfortunately I didn't have the parts he needed in stock here in America. So, I called the factory in England and was told of a newly built, nearly completed car awaiting payment and pick up by a German racing-team customer. I told them that actor/racing-team owner Jim Garner needed multiple sets of front and rear suspension components right away. They said they'd see what they could find. Garner kept calling me and was getting a little impatient, as the factory didn't have the replacement pieces he needed.

"So when it became apparent that the parts to repair Mr. Garner's car would be long delayed, I asked the Lola factory people about the car waiting for the German customer. They said that the pickup of and payment for the car were somewhat overdue and I told them that I needed all of the suspension off that new car to repair Mr. Garner's car."

The factory agreed, and dutifully stripped the new car of its suspension, sending it all to Todd on the West Coast. Todd recalls that the parts were sent to Dick Guldstrand's race shop in Culver City, California, which did the work; he visited the shop to help and oversee the work. "And we got 'Jimmy' Garner's Lola put back together."

James Garner Special

James Garner owned one other particularly interesting piece of four-wheeled hubris that could be included in any one of the following chapters about auto racing, but since he conceived and commissioned the car's build, I mention it here. On its nose it wore the name *James Garner Special,* although it has since been nicknamed "James Garner's Mystery Car." That's a bit of a misnomer because there isn't a lot of mystery to it. The *Special* was an Indy-style car with seating for a driver and outrigger seating just in front of the rear wheels, with room and vestigial windshields for two more.

The small-block Chevy V-8 was mounted in the back, in the style of then and now Indy car practice, with an odd roll protection and wing structure mounted just above the engine. This Pagoda-like bit of bodywork also contained two rectangular headlights, facing

James Garner may have been among the first to build a multi-seat, Indy-style race car, but others have advanced and continued the idea. This unusual tandem two-seater was built by the IZOD IndyCar series to help promote professional open-wheel racing. There is actually a pair of them, wearing different liveries, built from modified, lengthened, and strengthened Dallara chassis, powered by previous-generation naturally aspirated Honda Racing Indy V-8 engines. Enthusiasts and sponsors can buy laps in the rear passenger seat.

Here the car runs at Auto Club Speedway in Fontana, California. The author is in the rear seat, and all-time racing great Mario Andretti is at the wheel. The car has also been featured in a variety of Honda television commercials. *Photo Courtesy Mel Stone*

The *Special* is now owned, and is often displayed by, the Barber Motorsports Museum in Birmingham, Alabama. It appears almost in its original configuration, but sadly the name has been changed to *Barber's Special* and the paint color scheme has also been modified from the original. *Photo Courtesy Barber Motorsports Museum*

forward, although the car was anything but street legal. The wheels and tires were wide "knockoff"-style pieces and the car's hand-formed aluminum bodywork wrapped around them, with the engine's megaphone-style exhaust pipes poking out the back of the car. The body's prime color was white, with asymmetrical striping running down each side of the car; the stripes were blue down the right side of the car, and orange/red on the left.

In 2012, Jalopnik.com reported the following: "This show car was built around 1974. Mike Haas of Concord, California, was the owner and builder. Mike built show cars and painted rods at the time and my sense was that Mike built the car to tour the 'U.S. Show Circuit.'

"The race car chassis was stretched to accommodate the outboard seats as I recall. The engine was a small-block Chevy. The body was a work of art; almost all of the corners of the panels were formed in a radius. The workmanship was beautiful."

The Garner *Special* is currently owned by, and resides in, the Barber Motorsports Park Museum Collection in Birmingham, Alabama.

GMC Trucks

GMC was the official provider of trucks and support vehicles to Cherokee Productions for use in *The Rockford Files* (more detail in Chapter Five). Among them was a handsomely modified mid-1970s GMC pickup customized and used by James Garner for his personal use. Vista Group Public Relations handled product placement and public relations contracts for GMC (and sometimes Pontiac) at the time. The accounts were managed primarily by Eric Dahlquist, Sr., and Chuck Koch, both veteran journalists and magazine editors who segued into these aspects of the media business after long careers with *Motor Trend* and other publications.

Koch fondly recalls the good-looking red and maroon GMC, and a cherished working relationship with James Garner, whom he speaks of with obvious affection and respect: "I can't recall if that GMC was built specially for Garner, but I can't remember it being used on any other TV show or movie. I do know Garner drove it for a while and I'm pretty sure it appeared in at least one *Rockford* episode. As for it's final disposition, it would have gone to the GM auction, and been sold to a GM dealer.

"GMC did give him the one special Indy pace truck to drive for a while. I forget what year that was, but after Indy it was sent out here. We got a couple stories done on it and then Garner drove it for a while before it went back to GMC. That white truck was built to show up the pace car.

"The back story is that every year when a non-Chevy division of General Motors was chosen as the Speedway's pace car, that division always assumed GMC would provide the trucks, and that just went into their bid for the pace car program. However, no provision was ever made to recognize GMC for its contribution. That was part of the GM mentality of 'Oh, it's only trucks.' The Speedway always had a plentiful need for trucks (because

The body was a work of art; almost all of the corners of the panels were formed in a radius. The workmanship was beautiful.

GMC **WE'RE THE TRUCK PEOPLE!**

GMC played a major role in the transportation needs of James Garner's Cherokee Productions company during shooting of *The Rockford Files*. GMC commissioned its public relations firm to set up, shoot, and produce this poster showing the customized GMC often driven by James Garner (front) as personal transport, the famous "Rocky truck" driven by Jim Rockford's father in the series, and a grouping of GMC work trucks. *Photo Courtesy Vista Group*

they're so useful) and GMC often ended up supplying just as many, if not more, trucks than cars from the car division. But they didn't receive any real benefit in terms of publicity or TV coverage for doing so.

"One year GM senior exec John Rock decided to exact a measure of revenge and built one C1500 stepside ('fenderside' in GMC lingo) with a Corvette engine and special suspension. The idea was to blow off the official pace car that was, I think, a turbo Trans Am. Rock's hot rod truck did [just that]. Even though that act didn't gain any great amount of public exposure, except for the magazine articles we generated on the truck, it did allow GMC to walk around with its collective chest puffed out a bit for the month of May."

Unfortunately this special vehicle was completely destroyed in an accident that involved a fire; it did not involve James Garner in any way.

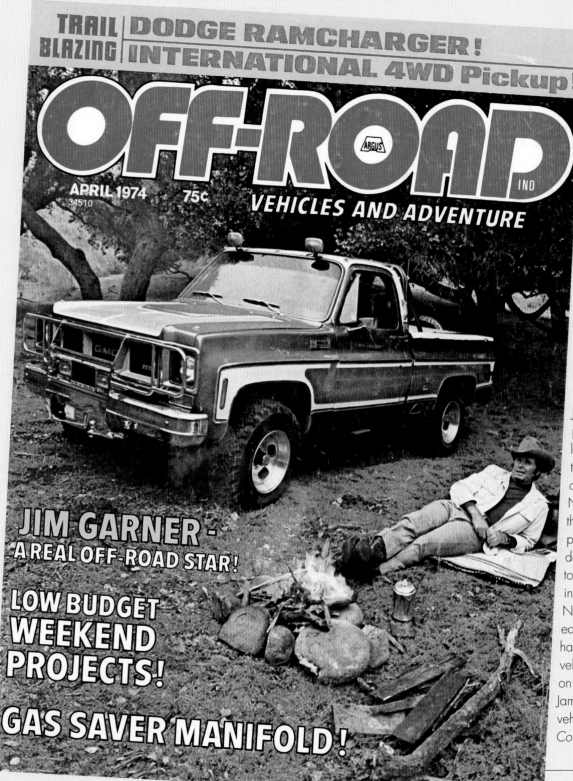

TRAIL BLAZING | **DODGE RAMCHARGER!** **INTERNATIONAL 4WD Pickup!**

OFF-ROAD

ARGUS IND

APRIL 1974 34510   **75¢**   VEHICLES AND ADVENTURE

JIM GARNER – A REAL OFF-ROAD STAR!

LOW BUDGET WEEKEND PROJECTS!

GAS SAVER MANIFOLD!

James Garner dressed up and posed in a very *Maverick*-like setting with the first GMC truck customized for him by off-roading legend Vic Hickey. Note the custom hood on this truck, a Hickey trademark piece, which was stepped down a few inches at the nose to increase forward visibility in tough off-roading situations. Naturally, automotive magazine editors were only too happy to have the handsome star and his vehicles featured prominently on their covers; guys like James Garner and the celebrity vehicles sell a lot of issues. *Photo Courtesy Tom Madigan Archive*

This is James and Lois Garner's current personal car, a 2009 Cadillac CTS. He takes great pride in his cars and most of them have been subtly customized or modified. "MAVROCK" wears factory paint with custom pinstriping and the owners' initials on each front door, aftermarket chrome-alloy wheels, a small hand-painted cherry on the rear deck (acknowledging the GM factory paint color, Black Cherry), and a very personalized license plate: MAV for Brett Maverick, and ROCK for Jim Rockford. *Photos Courtesy Jim Suva*

Garner had another GMC that he treated as his personal vehicle: a blue and white early 1970s GMC half ton that likely preceded the truck mentioned above. Retired GM racing engineer wizard Vic Hickey, whom James Garner got to know during his off-road racing days (see Chapter Three), customized it.

Vista Group's Eric Dahlquist doesn't remember a lot about this truck, since his company didn't put the deal together. He believes that because the truck wore a manufacturer's temporary license plate it was owned by General Motors and customized by Hickey, who, at the time, was running his own off-road parts and racing business, and who had his own promotional arrangements with General Motors. The front bumper with winch setup, special hood, roof-mounted driving lights, alloy wheels, and off-road tires are most consistent with Mr. Hickey's style of customization.

Trans Am

As the famous and much beloved character Jim Rockford, James Garner drove a Pontiac Firebird; it was an Esprit model, not the flashier, racier-looking Trans Am. However, a few years later, Garner himself owned a 1979 Firebird Trans Am.

In *The Garner Files*, and other published interviews, he describes a particularly unfortunate incident while driving the car home one night in January 1980. Garner was traveling on a particularly narrow, winding road through the Hollywood Hills when he was provoked into a dangerous bit of road rage fender tag by a seemingly crazed El Camino driver who apparently planned to rob him. Both drivers ultimately stopped to "take it outside" and fists flew, as did pointy-toed boots. Garner was battered, bruised, bloodied, and dazed; fortunately, his injuries weren't worse. The El Camino madman was arrested, convicted, and jailed.

Cadillac Sedan

Over time, a stream of nice cars has cycled its way through the Garner driveway and garage. Did he occasionally drive home one of *The Rockford Files'* Firebirds? Assuredly. Some of his personal vehicles are a black mid-1970s BMW 6 Series coupe, the newer Mini, and more recently a mildly personalized 2009 Cadillac CTS sedan.

The Caddy is painted a unique factory metallic shade called Black Cherry, with contrasting pinstriping (bearing the initials JG on the driver's door, and LG, for wife Lois Garner, on the passenger door). This car's not hard to spot around West Los Angeles or Malibu; the license plate, MAVROCK, is a bit of a giveaway.

The car appears mechanically stock, but wears 19-inch Lorenzo alloy wheels and low-profile tires, chrome-mesh Bentley-style front grilles, and tinted windows. Handsome, stealthy, and much more street legal than a Lola T70.

> Over time, a stream of nice cars has cycled its way through the Garner driveway and garage. Did he occasionally drive home one of *The Rockford Files'* Firebirds? Assuredly.

GRAND PRIX *The Movie*

James Garner as Pete Aron leads a pack of Formula One machines through Monza's storied high-bank turns. The massive rig-mounted Panavision camera needed to swivel itself level to accurately show the tilt of the cars on the banking. *Photo Courtesy MGM/Getty Images*

"Late in 1965, I heard that John Frankenheimer was about to direct a big-budget, CinemaScope feature about Formula One racing. I'd done a series of small films and felt I needed an 'epic.' . . .

— *James Garner*

The quote opposite is how James Garner opens the chapter in *The Garner Files* simply entitled "Racing." It only makes sense to allow him to complete the thought: "So, I had my agent get the script. I didn't know that Steve McQueen had already been signed for the part.

Chapter Two

"As it happened, Steve couldn't get along with the producer, Ed Lewis, so he backed out of the picture, flew to Taiwan to make *The Sand Pebbles* instead, and I got the part, even though [director John] Frankenheimer wanted an unknown to play [lead character] Pete Aron. I think he was looking for someone he could control. He had worked a lot with Burt Lancaster, and Burt always had an opinion. But both Lewis and the studio wanted me, and they overruled Frankenheimer."

Steve McQueen's version of this story doesn't match Garner's in every detail, but it is clear they were both circling around epic, big-budget motor racing films about the same time. McQueen was reportedly on cue to play a Formula One driver in a film named *Day of the Champion* and, of course, went on to produce and star in *Le Mans* in 1971. Regardless, Garner bagged the title role in the universally lauded *Grand Prix*, boasting a rich and capable international cast, fabulous scenery, and some of the most compelling and realistic racing cinematography ever captured on camera.

Director John Frankenheimer

The story of the making of *Grand Prix* has been well and often told, but needs to be fully understood to measure the impact it had on James Garner's life, career, car guy chops, and popularity as an actor. He wanted an epic; he certainly got one: "The movie follows

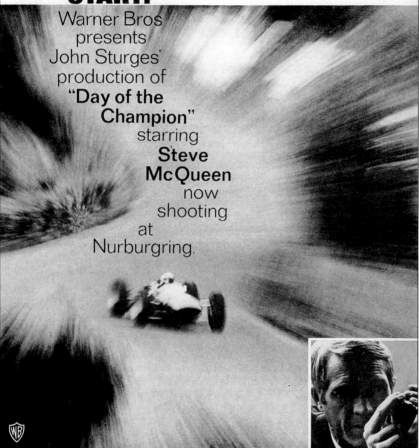

...OFF
TO A
ROARING
START.

Warner Bros
presents
John Sturges'
production of
"Day of the Champion"
starring
Steve McQueen
now
shooting
at
Nurburgring.

WB

Day of the Champion never actually had its day; the *Grand Prix* competitor ultimately became *Le Mans*. It wasn't long before everyone realized that two epic films about Grand Prix racing, starring two of America's favorite male movie stars, would create nothing but box office cannibalism. Frankenheimer and *Grand Prix*'s producers won the game, while Sturges and McQueen ended up basing their film on the world stage of endurance racing. *Photo Courtesy Matt Stone Collection*

four drivers through a season of racing for the world championship in the Grand Prix series. Antonio Sabato plays a promising rookie, Yves Montand a former champion at the end of his career, and Brian Bedford a Scotsman recovering from a crash. My character, Pete Aron, is an American trying to make a comeback after being thrown off his racing team for recklessly causing injury to a fellow driver. Eva Marie Saint, Jessica Walter, and Francoise Hardy play the love interests; the story is pure soap opera."

One can only wonder about some of the casting choices. It has been said that James Garner's role was loosely cast around American racing great, and then-current Formula One driver Dan Gurney; both are tall, particularly handsome, and equally all-American looking. Sabato's character could have resembled any number of young Italian Formula One upstarts at the time; Mr. Yamura was certainly riffed on Soichiro Honda, and Brian Bedford shows remarkable similarity to then-current Formula One ace Jim Clark.

The late John Frankenheimer was known as a somewhat uncompromising perfectionist, so there was little question that *Grand Prix*'s cinematography would be innovative and technically outstanding. It is; this film belongs in the movie library of every James Garner fan, and that of anyone who loves cars and motorsport. By the mid-1960s, motor racing had been portrayed in film numerous times, few of them to great effect. Little knowledge, skill, or equipment was available.

Racing was too often filmed with an actor sitting in a stationary car, with the action injected by projected racing footage running behind the actor. Naturally, it usually looked phony or contrived with little authenticity. There was no such thing as an "in-car camera." The size, bulk, and weight of 70- and 35-mm movie-quality camera equipment made it difficult to mount into a racing car for the capturing of real on-track action. Innovation and skillful cinematography were needed to capture the speed and immediacy of Grand Prix racing. It is no wonder then that the film was lauded and awarded for its innovation and technical achievement in terms of cinematography.

A cast for the ages and for the races: the *Grand Prix* dream team on the top row, from left to right are Enzo Fiermonte, Antonio Sabato, Adolfo Celi, Jack Watson, Brian Bedford, and Donal O'Brien. In the foreground, from left to right are Toshiro Mifune, James Garner, Eva Marie Saint, Jessica Walter, Francoise Hardy, Genevieve Page, and Yves Montand. The location is the front straight at Monza, still an important stop on the Formula One calendar, although its long, steeply banked corners (such an iconic element of Grand Prix action sequences) are no longer a part of the track configuration. *Photo Courtesy Everett Collection*

Among the many things that assured *Grand Prix*'s success was director John Frankenheimer's insistence on authenticity, plus his credibility as a filmmaker and sheer force of personality. Many of the day's Grand Prix greats had cameo roles in the film, and acted as racing consultants to the production. They include Joakim "Jo" Bonnier, Jack Brabham, Richie Ginther, Dan Gurney, Phil Hill (who often drove the specially modified Ford GT40 camera car), Graham Hill, Bruce McLaren, and others. Retired racing driver/car builder Carroll Shelby was officially credited as technical consultant. Noted racing photographer Bernard Cahier was an artistic, visual, and racing consultant on the production; he also portrayed a photojournalist in the film.

This is an alternate movie poster, also in Italian, for *Grand Prix*. Note the use of illustration instead of photography. Depicted from left are Eva Marie Saint, Yves Montand, Francoise Hardy, and James Garner. *Photo Courtesy Everett Collection*

The high-banked portion of Italy's *Autodromo Nazionale Monza* appears in several scenes in *Grand Prix*, but hasn't been used as part of the Formula One configuration since 1968. It did, however, provide a wonderful backdrop for a modern-day video documentary tribute to the great 1966 film, the man who starred in it, and a current champion.

James Garner visited the track in the late 1990s, and spent a "play date" out hooning around in a pair of 1960s-era Formula One machines with 1997 driving champion (and 1995 Indy 500 winner) Jacques Villeneuve. I don't know who produced this made-for-television video, but the narrator speaks with a clear British accent. Villeneuve also has considerable history with Formula One: His father, the late Gilles Villeneuve, was a driver in the 1980s for the Ferrari factory team, and a six-time Formula One winner.

Garner and Villeneuve clearly enjoyed meeting each other, driving together, and comparing and contrasting Formula One of the 1960s to modern times. Here's their conversation:

JV: *Grand Prix* was a great racing movie. Really showing the level of dangers and risk they were taking [back then].

JG: It was one of the most exhilarating experiences of my life, six months of driving those cars with the world's greatest drivers and circuits. You'd be surprised how fast you could learn when you have all the great drivers and circuits. We'd learn them three to four blocks at a time, and then be able to learn a whole circuit.

JV: I didn't feel like there was any point in doing it unless we did it in the real way, so we had the belts removed [from the cockpit] so it was more real. In today's race cars, you are very tight in the car; you don't move around in the cockpit even an inch. So to be in a car like this and move around [inside] much like a normal road car and be completely out in the open, you don't feel that secure.

At the time of this 1984 photo, young Jacques Villeneuve had yet to win the Indianapolis 500 or become Formula One World Champion.

Once you're there, you push it a bit and have some fun. It felt like a real race car, the engine wasn't too bad, and there was decent power in there. But I wasn't sure what would happen when I got sideways. It happened a few times but I wasn't going fast enough for it to be scary. They [the drivers back then] were taking more risks, but they weren't pushing the limit as much, because you paid dearly for it.

JG: I have a lot of great memories here.

JV: I had a blast!

Those iconic doors give this car away as a Ford GT40, but not a lot of it looks familiar from this viewpoint. GT40 chassis 1027 does yeoman duty as the *Grand Prix* camera car, with one of the large Panavision cameras mounted just forward of the left front wheel. The spare tire, which normally mounts in the nose, is also gone to make room for another camera that swivels, tilts, and rotates. The black boxes on the left side of the car appear to be battery boxes for operating the cameras and innovative swiveling heads. This configuration, sans front bodywork, was often used to film "lead and follow" sequences at relatively modest speeds, as the car's high-speed stability and aerodynamics would be highly compromised without the fenders and front hood. *Photo Courtesy Racing Icons*

Lead actors James Garner and Jessica Walter with one of the Formula racers used in *Grand Prix*. The car appears to be a McLaren, disguised to portray Pete Aron's "Yamura." The smiling young woman, mugging in Dad's helmet, is daughter Greta "Gigi" Garner. *Photo Courtesy Everett Collection*

Bob Bondurant speaks to an audience at a Petersen Automotive Museum screening of *Grand Prix*. At right is Evans Frankenheimer, wife of the late director John Frankenheimer. Mrs. Frankenheimer, herself an actress (born Evans Evans), also appears in the film, and was proud to tell the audience that there was no "green screen" or otherwise "phony photography" in the film, because her husband "wouldn't have it!" And of course this was long before the age of computer-generated imagery.

Frankenheimer's insistence on shooting live on location at the actual Grand Prix racetracks during Grand Prix race weekends added many layers of realism and complexity. Circuits featured in the film include Circuit de Monaco (Monaco), Clermont-Ferrand (France), Circuit de Spa-Francorchamps (Belgium), Circuit Park Zandvoort (Netherlands), Brands Hatch (United Kingdom), and Autodromo Nazionale Monza (Italy).

In addition, Frankenheimer visited the Ferrari factory and had an audience with Enzo Ferrari, to request to film on the Maranello grounds, and to use Ferrari cars and colors in the film. These locales were gorgeous, epic, and authentic; no phony back-screen projection photography here.

Bondurant recalls that director Frankenheimer had assembled a variety of footage that was to be used to sell the idea of *Grand Prix* to the studios and sponsors. "It was good exciting footage, but the timing was off," adds Bondurant "and the film and sound editing was all wrong. They had cars screaming through slow corners, but the engines were practically idling on fast straights. John asked me to sit in the booth and help re-edit the footage. Which we did and it came out fine: he got the green light and money from the studios to make the movie."

Bob Bondurant Training

Bob Bondurant speaks highly of James Garner as an actor, as a friend, and as a talented racing driver. "Prior to production, or any driver training, Frankenheimer asked me to take each of the four main actors out in a race car to see how they felt about the speed. I did, in a Shelby Cobra 289 race car. It was pretty easy to see who was going to be the star; who was the real racer among them.

"I don't think Brian Bedford even had a driver's license. He was obviously on edge and scared, as he'd never gone as fast in an automobile, and the notion of car control at high speed was totally new to him.

"Yves Montand seemed relatively comfortable; he was a middle-aged European with a fair amount of on-road driving experience, and likely had driven some hot sports cars, pretty fast, at one time or another.

"Antonio Sabato was somewhere in the middle, not as petrified as Bedford was, but obviously he hadn't had much experience behind the wheel of an automobile, particularly a race car at high speeds.

"But James Garner was a natural. While gunning around in the Cobra, I looked over at him and the faster we went the bigger he smiled. He was having fun, but he was also paying attention. He was watching my lines through the corners, shifting points, and braking points; already learning how to race. He asked smart questions, and obviously couldn't wait to get behind the wheel of a car and really start working."

High-performance driver training always begins in the classroom, likely in front of a chalkboard, with discussion of racing lines, apexes, and how to enter and exit corners for

Bob Bondurant rides shotgun in a Shelby GT350 as a grinning James Garner drives. Bondurant said from the beginning that James Garner enjoyed driving and racing from the word "go" and had the attitude and mentality of a professional racing driver. *Photo Courtesy Bondurant School*

maximum speed and minimum lap times. James Garner's training with Bob Bondurant at Southern California's Willow Springs Raceway began no differently.

They made videos of Garner and Bondurant gathered around a chalkboard talking their way around Willow Springs. Then they went out together in a Shelby GT350 Mustang, first with Bondurant at the wheel, then switching places, learning the lines, shift points, and braking points. Bondurant was pleased with his capable student. "Jim caught on fast," Bondurant recalls. "And he thinks like a racer. He paid attention and asked smart questions. After some time together in the same car, we separated and each drove our own car

Bondurant comments that James Garner was a model student, who listened to the instructor's advice and worked hard to improve his driving skills. The two remain friends today. *Photo Courtesy Bondurant School*

Bob Bondurant had to do a little selling to Formula One car owners to get one to loan him a car for Garner to train in. He finally found an owner that believed and trusted that Garner had "the right stuff" to drive his Lotus.
Photo Courtesy Bondurant School

and played lead and follow," first with Bondurant in the lead car, with Garner behind and watching his lines and technique, then switching so the teacher could critique the student.

It wasn't long before Garner progressed to faster machinery. After the Shelby Mustang, and a brief progression of smaller open-wheeled racers, it was soon time for him to hone his skills aboard a real Formula One racer.

Bondurant recalls having to negotiate and do some convincing with a couple of car owners, in his attempts to borrow or rent a car for Garner to practice in; several questioned the need and sense of sending an inexperienced actor out in one of these machines. They

As you can see in this photo, James Garner, about 6 feet 3 inches, sat a little tall in a Formula One racer. American racing great Dan Gurney, at around the same height, had the same problem. You can see quite a bit of Mr. Garner's torso in this shot, and you notice that the rear roll bar and helmet pad, which should sit at about the middle of his helmet, are actually a little too close to his neck.
Photo Courtesy Bondurant School

ended up using a Lotus, and Bondurant assured the owner that James Garner would start out slowly, come up to speed gradually, and could absolutely handle the car. And he did!

Bondurant faced a challenge when it came to the other drivers. Early on, racing driver Jim Russell was engaged to help train the actors to drive in the film. Bondurant was sure he was empowered and instructed to do the same, and after a friendly meeting with Russell, they worked out an accord: Bondurant's prime responsibility would remain James Garner, and Russell would pay more attention to the others.

Cinematography and Film Design

Capturing the speed, essence, danger, and beauty of Formula One racing was a challenge, but *Grand Prix*'s innovative director, editing team, and a masterful group of cinematographers were clearly up to the challenge. Cameraman John M. Stephens was often assigned the task of shooting out of a helicopter following the action. Stephens sometimes worked in white or light-colored pants and sneakers, and recalls that by the end of most days his shoes and pants were stained green from flying so close to treetops. Stephens also liberally credits Frick Enterprises for the development of the various innovative camera mounts used to attach the large Panavision cameras to the variety of race and chase cars used during filming.

Stephens was interviewed and featured in the *Valley Sun Newspaper* in June 2013, which said that his big break came on the Oscar-winning *Grand Prix*. "The picture won an Academy Award for its special effects and it was the electronic pan-and-tilt–head camera I invented that got those close-ups of James Garner driving around the track at 160 mph."

It was 1965; director Frankenheimer refused to shoot slow cars and speed up the film, as had been the norm. He approached Stephens and said, "How would you like to be the cameraman going 180 mph in a specially built camera car while photographing the actual drivers on the Grand Prix circuit?"

"It would scare the hell out of me," replied Stephens. Instead he devised the first radio-controlled remotely operated camera head, which captured the thrill of the race from inside the race, capable of producing never-before-seen shots, such as panning from James Garner's face to Brian Bedford coming up right behind him while speeding along at close to 200 mph. All the while, Stephens was able to view the footage via a remote monitor in the relative safety of a helicopter hovering a few hundred feet above the racetrack.

It's hard to describe just how breathtaking those hair-raising race scenes are, and you'll just have to check out the movie to appreciate the full extent of Stephens' ingenuity. It's easy to connect the dots between Stephens' time on skis barreling down Bald Mountain with camera in hand, to the incredible action shots he devised.

The specially modified mid-engine Ford GT40 racing prototype is particularly interesting. It was converted to a camera car; it carried a large robotic, remote-control Panavision camera in the front trunk area that was capable of keeping up with the Formula One machines while on track.

Grand Prix ace action cameraman John M. Stephens, Bob Bondurant, and Evans Frankenheimer address a *Grand Prix* screening audience at Los Angeles' Petersen Automotive Museum in 2013.

"How would you like to be the cameraman going 180 mph in a specially built camera car while photographing the actual drivers on the Grand Prix circuit?"

Phil Hill and Bob Bondurant were no strangers to Ford's all-conquering GT40 racer, so it's not a huge surprise that a modified GT40 was used as a high-speed camera car for capturing on-track action in the making of *Grand Prix*. Curiously enough, Steve McQueen's Solar Productions company also used a highly modified GT40 for similar duty in the making of his motorsport epic, *Le Mans*, a few years later.

The GT40 pictured here (chassis 1027), as used during the filming of *Grand Prix*, is a fairly early GT40 chassis, as it does not carry some of the aerodynamic updates the model received along the way. Later GT40s replaced these knock-off wire wheels with wider, stronger alloys. This car has in fact traded hands several times since its use in the making of *Grand Prix*, and has since been restored, painted yellow, and retrofitted with the later alloy wheels.

The Panavision camera in the nose could sweep several hundred degrees to capture action on either side of the car; notice a bundle of cable controls that allowed the passenger/camera operator to sweep the camera and turn it on and off. The camera and motorized rotating head added more than 100 pounds to the weight of the front of the car, and certainly diminished its top speed and aerodynamics considerably. However, it was still fast enough to keep up with the 1.5-liter Grand Prix cars and smaller-engined Formula Three cars driven by the *Grand Prix* actors. *Photo Courtesy Pat Brollier/Source Interlink Media/Getty Images*

Setting Authenticity

Frankenheimer's insistence that the rented, begged, and borrowed Formula cars used for the staged scenes look as much as possible like the current, 1966 season cars, allowed for some masterful editing. In several of the race scenes, the green flag start and early lap sequences are from the real race. Using proper-looking cars allowed the crew to come back and shoot alternative starts, passing scenes, accidents, and of course, their own finishes according to the plot and script. It takes an eagle-eyed expert to spot which is which, because the cars, liveries, even exhaust pipes all matched as closely as possible.

Many of the cars used by the production to create its own scenes were not only outdated Formula One machines, but also slightly smaller and less powerful Formula Three racers. Some, more successfully than others, were dressed up to look like the current top-tier cars. This added countless layers of complexity and cost to the crews' job in preparing

This staged pre-grid scene from *Grand Prix* is about as authentic looking as it could be. Actor Yves Montand (left) prepares to board his Ferrari, while James Garner (right) does the same with his "Yamura." The track location is historic Brands Hatch in England, often the locale of the British Grand Prix. *Photo Courtesy MGM/Getty Images*

All photos by Mike George

The Shelby GT350H (Hertz) Mustang is among the more storied models produced by Shelby American. The H model was the epicenter of a promotional program by Hertz car rental company to inject some pizzazz into the notion of jet-set travel and making your rental car an exciting part of the travel experience. The program's first year was 1966, the second year of Shelby GT350 production. Most of the cars were painted black with bright metallic gold stripes, in keeping with Hertz' corporate color scheme. About 1,000 of this model were built, the first 80 or so equipped with 4-speed manual transmissions, and the rest of the run using 3-speed automatics.

It seems that some number of the high-powered business execs who wanted to rent them didn't know how to drive a stick, or just didn't want to. And many of the weekend racer types who rented them burned up a few clutches and transmissions along the way, so the automatic transmission was the safer and likely less costly choice for the company. The GT350H was thus nicknamed the "Hertz Rent-A-Racer" because so many were reputedly rented then raced over the weekend; evidence of temporary roll bars and racing harness–style seatbelts showed when the given car was returned to Hertz on Monday morning.

Urban legend also maintains that more than a few were returned to the rental lot with the fresh 289 Hi-Po V-8 having been replaced by a tired, garden-variety, low-performance Mustang or Falcon engine after a weekend engine swap. Few Hertz renters will confirm or deny.

Black with gold striping was the most common and popular color combination for the Hertz-spec Shelby, although red and green with either gold or white stripes were among alternate choices. The H model was otherwise mechanically identical to the standard GT350, including a high-performance 289-ci V-8, upgraded wheels and tires, and high-performance suspension.

Looking every bit as a proper GT350H should, Shelby 6S611, forever famous for its appearances in *Grand Prix*, and as James Garner and Bob Bondurant's ride all around Europe during that Summer of 1966, sits just right on its proper steel Magnum 500 wheels. After use in the film, the car has been resold several times, having lived a while in Germany, with its rear end jacked up on spring shackle extensions, and wearing aftermarket aluminum mag wheels. The car has been fully and properly restored, and now lives in the northeastern United States.

The car used during the filming of *Grand Prix*, Shelby chassis number 6S611, was built in late 1965 and pressed immediately into service in Europe. According to the Shelby American Automobile Club (SAAC) Registry, James Garner, in 2005, confirmed to them that this car was born and driven as a 4-speed example. Its original invoice price to Hertz was $3,547, plus $105.55 for chrome Magnum 500 wheels, plus an additional $420.22 to cover the cost of an AM radio, power brakes, pre-delivery prep, and freight charges. Quite a car for $3,899.70.

The 306-horse 289 looks just right, subject to immaculate and authentic restoration. Clamps, hoses, wiring, Koni shocks, aluminum intake, and even the "red cap" Autolite battery are as they should be. Note the factory shock tower brace that stiffens and triangulates the shock towers and firewall.

The "Grand Prix" GT350H was well equipped; note the factory 4-speed manual shifter, whereas most Hertz cars were automatics. The wood-rimmed Shelby wheel and dash-mounted Rotunda tach are as they should be too. Factory air conditioning was an unusual find on many cars in Europe in the mid-1960s, but of course the filming of the movie took place during hotter months and the car was all black, so it would have been a bit uncomfy for its star driver and driving instructor without A/C.

You may wonder how to quickly tell a 1965 Shelby GT350 from a 1966. In terms of Hertz rental models, that's easy, as there was no Hertz rental car or program in 1965. The other quick tell of a 1966 is that the 1965s still had metal vent panels in the rear sail panel, whereas 1966 Shelby Mustangs had the attractive quarter windows, as seen on the "Grand Prix" GT350H.

Upon delivery to Hi-Performance Motors in El Segundo, California, the car was shipped to Germany to begin work on the film. The choice of this car seems most appropriate, since Carroll Shelby was credited as the technical consultant for *Grand Prix*. In addition, Shelby American team driver Bob Bondurant trained James Garner at Willow Springs Raceway in California using a nearly identical Shelby GT350. The car not only served as Bondurant and Garner's personal transportation around Europe during the filming of *Grand Prix*, but 6S611 makes several cameo appearances in the movie, seen trolling through, or parked in, the pits and paddock in several scenes.

One of its more prominent scenes is when Pete Aron (Garner), stops to chat with Pat Stoddard (Jessica Walter); she leans into the passenger window to talk, and the interior of the car, with its 4-speed manual shifter, is clearly visible. SAAC quotes James Garner as saying that he drove the Shelby to the Monte Carlo Casino and parked it among the Ferraris and Maseratis, and that people flocked around it, ignoring the other cars.

After completion of the film, the Mustang was sold in Europe and stayed there for several years with a number of owners. It has since been purchased by a private collector and has been fully restored to factory-original condition; it is now stateside.

Shelby greatly simplified the grille treatment on all first-generation GT350s. The iconic, chromed "horse and corral" are gone, and the grille is devoid of ornamentation, with the exception of the small "running horse" badge on the driver's side. The GT model's grille-mounted fog/driving lights were also not factory installed on GT350s.

Even though the Hertz black-with-gold-stripes livery isn't the only factory color combination you see on a GT350H, it is the most common, and by far the most popular among collectors. It proved so strongly identified with the Hertz/Shelby Rent-A-Racer program that when Shelby, Ford, and Hertz reprised the program in 2006, they built only coupes, and they were available only in black with gold stripes. The model was renamed the GT-H (without the "350") and the program continued in 2007 on a smaller scale with a run of convertibles, painted white with silver stripes.

A contemplative James Garner (far left), as Pete Aron, appears to be psyching up for a race. James Garner famously said that "the acting is done in the pits" and not in the car at speed. This great period photo emphasizes his height compared to the compact Formula machine. *Photo Courtesy Terry O'Neill/Getty Images*

James Garner (left), as Formula One journeyman driver Pete Aron, looks focused and ready to race in this pit shot from *Grand Prix*. Here he has with him everything a driver needed at the time to be cockpit ready: his racing suit, his gloves, his own steering wheel, and his red, white, and blue helmet. *Photo Courtesy Everett Collection*

the cars, but increased Frankenheimer's editing and flexibility manyfold. This is one of the key elements that make *Grand Prix* "work."

James Garner worked hard to earn credibility with the "real" racing drivers, which he did. In his autobiography, he tells the story of doing "a choreographed shot with five or six cars passing and jockeying and when we cut, we'd all turn around and race back. Fuuuuuun!"

A variety of camera rigging and filmmaking techniques were used to get the footage to look just right. There was at least one "car rig" built to be towed behind the camera car for certain high-speed sequences. Montand and Bedford are both seen in this contraption, as Bedford never got comfortable with the high speeds. Frankenheimer admitted that Brian had to be photographed in the rig, at lower speeds, or doubled by another driver.

When it came to those Formula One machines, the production got a bit of a break because the series was switching racing engine formulas at just that time, from 1.5-liter to 3.0-liter naturally aspirated power plants, so the 1.5-liter machines were outmoded by the

One of the many cinemagraphic aspects that makes *Grand Prix* so good is the superb and innovative camera work that captures the action as realistically as possible. Cameraman John M. Stephens commented that some of the original mount systems were almost too good, eliminating any notion of camera shake, which took away some of the drama and tension of the high-speed passages. The cinematographers re-engineered the mounts to allow a bit more of the cars' natural shake and buzz to filter through to the camera; it amps up the look and speed in an organic way. This scene was shot at Monaco. *Photo Courtesy Rainer W. Schlegelmilch/Getty Images*

Notable Quotables from the Making of *Grand Prix*

Note the Italian text on this theater poster for *Grand Prix*. The inset photos (clockwise from top left) portray James Garner, Eva Marie Saint, Yves Montand, Francoise Hardy, Jessica Walter, and Brian Bedford. *Photo Courtesy Matt Stone Collection*

Two tall, American racing greats, Dan Gurney and James Garner, share laughs and story swapping at an oil company party in the late 1970s. *Photo Courtesy AAR Archive*

Much of the background and back story on the epic filming of *Grand Prix* is covered in the documentary "The Making of *Grand Prix*," which is filled with notable comments from John Frankenheimer, James Garner, John M. Stephens, and many others from the cast, crew, and world of motorsport. Here are a few favorites:

When I look back, I don't know how the hell we ever did that film. —John Frankenheimer

Somehow we made it work, and you have to hand it to Frankenheimer for pushing, pushing, pushing people to get it done. —James Garner

He definitely broke ground, in that he made the commitment to film real racing under real conditions. —Dan Gurney

I always loved cars. I started racing, and then realized I didn't have the talent. —John Frankenheimer

When you're in a Formula car, or any race car, you don't worry about acting. You concentrate on your braking and your turning points, and just driving. We do our acting in the pits. —James Garner

Frankenheimer was tough, hard on people, but a genius. —James Garner

Steve McQueen waited about a year to see Grand Prix. When his son Chad finally made him take him to see it—he was my next-door neighbor, remember—he stopped by and told me, "Yeah, pretty good picture. Pretty good." Coming from Steve, it was high praise. —James Garner

Adding another splash of elegance to the filming of *Grand Prix* in Monaco were HSH Prince Rainier III and his wife, Princess Grace, with James Garner. *Photo Courtesy Mondadori Portfolio via Getty Images*

Handsome and elegant Japanese actor Toshiro Mifune portrays industrialist and racing team owner/car builder Izo Yamura. It is said that this name was made up as a spin on the Japanese industrial firm Yamaha. Mr. Yamura gives Pete Aron a break when his luck is really down, and invites him to the Yamura shop to be fitted for his new race car. *Photo Courtesy Camerique/Getty Images*

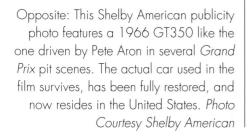

Opposite: This Shelby American publicity photo features a 1966 GT350 like the one driven by Pete Aron in several *Grand Prix* pit scenes. The actual car used in the film survives, has been fully restored, and now resides in the United States. *Photo Courtesy Shelby American*

new rules, and available for use by the *Grand Prix* producers, at substantial rental fees, no doubt. Hence the small-engined 1965-season cars were modified to look like, as much as possible, the current 1966-season cars running the series during filming.

There was no such doubling needed for James Garner, who did all his own driving, high-speed and otherwise. When the script called for his character, Pete Aron, to be involved in a wreck at Monaco, with the driver and car crashing into the ocean, it really is Garner in the water, swimming for shore and medical attention. In a scene in which Aron's car catches fire, Garner insisted on driving the stunt even with the back of his car belching huge flurries of flame.

So many factors contribute to the greatness of *Grand Prix*, not only to car and racing enthusiasts, but also to general audiences as an elegant, epic, lushly depicted story. Saul

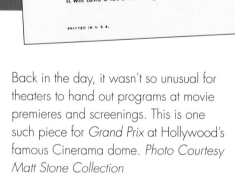

Back in the day, it wasn't so unusual for theaters to hand out programs at movie premieres and screenings. This is one such piece for *Grand Prix* at Hollywood's famous Cinerama dome. *Photo Courtesy Matt Stone Collection*

Bass was known as an innovative film designer, and he created the many unique montage sequences, particularly notable in the film's opening scenes.

The score was composed and conducted by the already-legendary Maurice Jarre. One of his great touches is that the background music for each race is entirely different. This is also echoed in the visuals: one race is depicted only in high-speed action, another is seen in slow motion, and yet another focuses only on spectators and people.

Classic and collector car fans will love watching *Grand Prix* today because many of the scenes are filled with some of the most desirable cars of the day. Racetrack-pit sequences brim with a variety of Ferraris and other now highly sought after exotica. In addition, the

THE CAST

PETE ARON	JAMES GARNER
LOUISE FREDERICKSON	EVA MARIE SAINT
JEAN-PIERRE SARTI	YVES MONTAND
IZO YAMURA	TOSHIRO MIFUNE
SCOTT STODDARD	BRIAN BEDFORD
PAT	JESSICA WALTER
NINO BARLINI	ANTONIO SABATO
LISA	FRANCOISE HARDY
AGOSTINI MANETTA	ADOLFO CELI
HUGO SIMON	CLAUDE DAUPHIN
GUIDO	ENZO FIERMONTE
MONIQUE DELVAUX SARTI	GENEVIEVE PAGE
JEFF JORDAN	JACK WATSON
WALLACE BENNETT	DONAL O'BRIEN
CHILDREN'S FATHER	JEAN MICHAUD
SURGEON	ALBERT REMY
MRS. STODDARD	RACHEL KEMPSON
MR. STODDARD	RALPH MICHAEL
SPORTSCASTERS	ALAN FORDNEY
	ANTHONY MARSH
	TOMMY FRANKLIN
	PHIL HILL
TIM RANDOLPH	GRAHAM HILL
BOB TURNER	BERNARD CAHIER
JOURNALIST	

THE CREDITS

Screen Story and Screenplay by ROBERT ALAN AURTHUR
Directed by JOHN FRANKENHEIMER
Produced by EDWARD LEWIS
Music Composed and Conducted by MAURICE JARRE
A JOHN FRANKENHEIMER FILM
Presented by METRO-GOLDWYN-MAYER
In SUPER PANAVISION® and METROCOLOR

Director of Photography	LIONEL LINDON, A.S.C.
Production Designer	RICHARD SYLBERT
Supervising Film Editor	FREDRIC STEINKAMP
Film Editors	HENRY BERMAN
	STEWART LINDER
	FRANK SANTILLO
	ENRICO ISACCO
Assistant Director	GORDON DANIELS
Sound Editor	MILT RICE
Special Effects	FRANK AGNONE
Property Master	GIULIANO LAURENTI
Make-up	ALFIO MENICONI
Costumes Selected and Supervised by and Hair Styles and Make-Up Created by	SYDNEY GUILAROFF
United Production Manager	WILLIAM KAPLAN
Production Managers	SACHA KAMENKA
Monaco & France	SAM GORODISKY
Italy	PETER CROWHURST
England	FRANKLIN MILTON
Sound Recording	ROY CHARMAN
	PHIL HILL
Racing Advisers	JOAKIM BONNIER
	RICHIE GINTHER
Racing Camera Mounts Executed by	FRICK ENTERPRISES
Technical Consultant	CARROLL SHELBY
Second Unit Cameramen	JOHN M. STEPHENS
	JEAN-GEORGES FONTENELLE
	YANN LE MASSON
Visual consultant; montages, titles by	SAUL BASS

JAMES GARNER   EVA MARIE SAINT   YVES MONTAND   TOSHIRO MIFUNE   BRIAN BEDFORD   JESSICA WALTER   ANTONIO SABATO   FRANCOISE HARDY

costuming and fashion are pure Europe in the 1960s. Pete Aron drove a very special automobile: a now-rare and expensive black-and-gold 1966 Shelby GT350H.

One of the 10-highest-grossing films of 1966, *Grand Prix* won three Academy Awards for its technical achievements, and critical reviews were generally spectacular. Reviewer Bosley Crowther called the film "a smashing and thundering compilation of racing footage shot superbly at the scenes of the big meets around the circuit, jazzed up with some great photographic trickery ... Mr. Frankenheimer belts

The inside of this original *Grand Prix* screening program lists *Grand Prix* cast, crew, executives, and creative team as well as including headshots of all the stars. *Photo Courtesy Matt Stone Collection*

you with such a barrage of magnificent shots of the racing cars, seen from every angle and every possible point of intimacy, that you really feel as though you've been in it after you've seen this film.

"Furthermore, the director and Saul Bass fill that mammoth screen from time to time with multiple graphics and montages that look like movies at a world's fair. Triple and quadruple panels and even screen-filling checkerboards . . . hit the viewer with stimulations that optically generate a sort of intoxication with racing. It's razzle-dazzle of a random sort, but it works."

When Cinerama, Incorporated, developed its ultra-widescreen Cinerama movie format and cameras in the early 1960s, it was as big a deal, when Imax or 3-D revolutionized movie going and filmmaking some years later. The company designed a special theater building to house the huge screen and maximize the impact of the format's enhanced sound quality, based on Buckminster Fuller's unique geodesic dome principle. The original Hollywood Cinerama Theater opened in the fall of 1963; the first movie premiered there was Stanley Kramer's film *Its A Mad, Mad, Mad, Mad World*, which opened the Cinerama Dome on November 7, 1963.

The property, currently named Pacific's Cinerama Theater, has been nicknamed the Cinerama Dome since the beginning, and is located at 6360 Sunset Boulevard in Hollywood, California. The domed roof consists of about 300 pre-cast cement panels, each weighing more than 3,000 pounds. The Cinerama Dome has been home to many glittering Hollywood film premieres, and has shown *Grand Prix* numerous times.

Film company marketers have had good creative fun with the building's unique shape; during the showing of various *Spiderman* movies, Spidey himself has been seen crawling down the dome. It has also been decorated in green "skin" and adorned with horns honoring *Shrek* when one of that franchise's films was showing there.

The famous theater was designated Los Angeles Historic–Cultural Monument No. 659 on December 18, 1998.

However, Crowther concluded "the big trouble with this picture . . . is that the characters and their romantic problems are stereotypes and clichés . . . You come away with the feeling that you've seen virtually everything there is to see in Grand Prix racing, except the real guys who drive those killer cars."

After such a glowing review, it's somewhat ironic that Mr. Crowther's final statement isn't wholly true, because you *do* see many of the "real guys who drive those killer cars," which is an important element of the film's authenticity.

If you love cars, racing, and are any sort of James Garner fan, the movie belongs in your library. In his autobiography, James Garner commented that making *Grand Prix* was about the most fun thing he's ever done, which isn't hard to imagine.

He also said, "If I hadn't been an actor, I'd like to have been a race driver."

Which also isn't hard to imagine.

James Garner is the model of concentration during driver training exercises with Bob Bondurant at Willow Springs in 1965. And how about those split prism goggles, likely military-spec pieces? Of course "billed" helmets and these goggles have long since been replaced by much safer full-face helmets, which hadn't yet made the scene when *Grand Prix* was filmed. *Photo Courtesy Bondurant School*

James Garner and Scooter Patrick look poised for action in their No. 59 Bill Stroppe–prepared and –entered Ford Bronco. This photo must have been taken early in the race, as the car and both drivers still appear clean and free of dust and mud. The presence of the boom microphone seen at the lower right of the photo indicates that the team was likely being interviewed on television, or perhaps for the filming of *The Racing Scene* documentary. All of the Ford Stroppe Team Broncos were constructed in Stroppe and Son's Long Beach, California, race shop. *Photo Courtesy Tom Madigan Archive*

DIRTY DANCING *Off-Road Racing*

"I got up at 4:00 in the morning to do this. My buddy Scooter Patrick and I are going to race this Bronco about 850 miles through hot dry desert, mountains, sand, and what have you, all the way from Ensenada to La Paz in Baja California. We'll be eating dust for about 24 hours, and coughing it up for two weeks. If you ask me if I'm a little crazy for doing this, you'd probably get one of these [shakes head up and down]. If you ask me if we think we can go down the road quicker than 300 other guys, I'd probably say 'we're sure as hell going to find out . . .'

— *James Garner, prior to the start of the 1968 Baja 1000 off-road race*

om Madigan is a long-time racer, racing writer, book author, and magazine editor. His books, magazine stories, and anecdotes have a legitimate "been there, done that" gravitas to them because, when big things happened in motorsport during the 1960s and 1970s, Madigan was there covering the events. He got to know the players: car company execs and engineers, race team members, and of course, the drivers. He knew James Garner, Steve McQueen, and Paul Newman personally; he attended road-racing school with Newman. Madigan witnessed firsthand the birth of modern off-road racing in the 1960s, and also edited several magazines dedicated to the sport and motorsport of off-roading.

Chapter Three

Madigan recalls, "James Garner and Steve McQueen got into off-road racing. One of the main reasons they got into it was that back then off-road racing wasn't as stressful as road racing, there was a lot less practice, and it wasn't a huge time commitment like competitive road racing. It also didn't cost as much to race off-road. In addition, most of the studio types and their insurance carriers didn't think it was 'real' racing. Garner and McQueen were both superstar hero-type guys in the movies and for some reason, their bosses didn't seem to object to it as much as they did when a big star wanted to go road-racing in a sports car."

The Birth of Off-Roading

Off-roading grew in America during the 1950s as a byproduct of World War II because so many soldiers drove Jeeps and other four-wheel-drive rigs in the war, and enjoyed it when there weren't bombs falling around them. Many of those discharged GIs brought Jeeps home with them, or bought them used as army surplus, and began playing with them as recreational toys.

In the early 1960s, motorcycle dealer/racer/stuntman Bud Ekins and his brother Dave spent considerable time exploring Mexico's

Baja 500 action from 1972: Garner and co-driver Slick Gardner ran this Bill Stroppe Ford pickup; they ran well and finished. So many of Stroppe's great speed and durability tricks lie beneath the skin of this relatively stock-looking F-100. Note the virtually unmodified bodywork and relatively unexotic aluminum "slot mag" wheels. The use of two hood pins per side made sure the hood didn't rattle, fly up into the windshield, or end up in the desert. *Photo Courtesy Tracksidephoto.com*

The Garner/Gardner Stroppe F-100 slides and claws its way through the 1972 Baja 500; the trucks were in fact highly modified, although looked relatively tame on the outside. Today's tube-framed mid-engined "Trophy Trucks" were still a thing of the future. The roll bar was a somewhat simple affair, as was the add-on lighting; note that this truck still runs its period California license plate, as it was probably still street legal. *Photo Courtesy Tracksidephoto.com*

Baja Peninsula on motorcycles. Shortly thereafter, Southern California automotive designer Bruce Meyers invented the dune buggy, and Meyers and friends spent some time testing the viability of this flyweight, fiberglass-bodied buggy in Mexico. It wasn't long before various promoters began hosting and promoting off-roading events.

Jeep racer and enterprising off-roading pioneer Brian Chuchua helped off-road racing grow through his support and participation in the sport. In 1965 he hosted the National Four-Wheel-Drive Grand Prix, the first modern off-road race staged for spectators, held in the Santa Ana River bed in Riverside, California. It was part race and part off-roading obstacle course, and was designed to display vehicles' and drivers' off-road prowess. Garner and McQueen both competed there.

In 1967, off-road racing was organized and sanctioned; its first big-time event was the Mexican 1000 off-road race, later renamed the Baja 1000. A shorter version born shortly thereafter was the Baja 500. The original Baja 1000 route explored the desolate beach and desert wilderness along an approximately 1,000-kilometer route from Ensenada to La Paz. Racing on the dirt in Mexico wasn't an entirely new proposition, as the Carrera Panamericana of the 1950s was an important stop on the international road-racing schedule.

The National Off Road Racing Association (NORRA) provides this bit of history: "Ed Pearlman is the man who first organized the Mexican 1000, co-founded NORRA and founded the Off-Road Motorsports Hall of Fame [ORMHOF].

This horse-collar-shaped foam-filled ring was a very early and rudimentary version of today's head and neck shoulder support device HANS; and it also helped protect the driver's neck and shoulders from being cut or wear-burned by the racing harness shoulder belts. No one knows of course what Mr. Garner was thinking or saying at this moment, but you can almost hear his seminal character, Jim Rockford, saying, "Oh, come on guys, do I really have to wear this? It looks dumb." *Photo Courtesy Tracksidephoto.com*

Saddled up and ready to ride are James Garner at the wheel and co-pilot Don Adams, a well-seasoned off-road racer. Note the wear and tear on Adam's helmet vs. Garner's much fresher looking Simpson. Goggles were a must, as the Jeep's vestigial "windshield" was made of clear plastic and only about 8 inches tall, offering minimum dust, rock, and mud protection if any. *Photo Courtesy Tracksidephoto.com*

Garner goes a little "Dan Gurney" on entertainer and fellow racer Dick Smothers, who won the race. Photographer Jim Ober said it was one of the most exciting races he'd ever witnessed at Riverside International Raceway. Smothers drove Jeep No. 2 that day, while Garner's mount was No. 1, although they finished in the opposite order. The reason for the Gurney reference is that even though the champagne shower is now a common victory podium tradition, Gurney is credited with inventing the move when he and A. J. Foyt won the 24 Hours of Le Mans in 1967 in a Ford GT Mk IV. *Photo Courtesy Tracksidephoto.com*

Garner congratulates fellow celebrity Dick Smothers on a hard-fought win at the Jeep-only closed-course off-road race in 1978, driving matched Jeep CJs. The pair represented Hollywood's considerable driving talent, with Smothers nipping Garner for the win. *Photo Courtesy Tracksidephoto.com*

His legacy of contributions to the development of off-road motorsports is undeniable. He served in the Pacific theater during World War II as a Marine. During his time in Guam he organized fun Jeep races for the troops to help keep up morale. When he returned from the war he purchased a surplus Jeep and spent three months touring through Baja finding fishing spots. He and his wife, Shirley, opened a chain of flower shops in the San Fernando Valley, California, but by the 1950s off-road exploration and fly-fishing still interested him greatly. In the early 1960s he began racing for fun at the Riverside off-road events hosted by Brian Chuchua.

"In 1966, Don Francisco joined Ed Pearlman and a group of other California-based off-road enthusiasts to co-found NORRA. Francisco helped establish the inaugural Mexican 1000 in 1967. Utilizing his skills as a pilot, Francisco charted a viable race course and calculated needed service stop locations. Using his personal aircraft, specially modified to fly on lower-octane pump gas, Don was very active during the actual events transporting VIPs and press up and down the race course. He also worked with Pearlman to establish the first set of rules and classes for the sport of off-road racing.

"Another reason I believe that off-road racing appealed to big game actors, such as James Garner, was that it's a terribly macho activity: man against machine, man and machine against the elements, and of course the whole thing was very competitive on all levels. And the race cars were fun; odd combinations of trucks, buggies, Volkswagens (what we now call SUVs), and even passenger cars jacked up to the sky for

ground clearance running huge V-8 engines for power. Wild and wooly days."

James Garner describes the vibe in his autobiography: "It's an eerie, majestic, untamed landscape where the terrain changes suddenly and drastically, going from seaside to desert, mountains to cactus forest, silt marsh to lava field. There's every road hazard you can imagine: auto parts, fenders, and tires litter the course. There are steep grades, sharp switchbacks, rocks, washouts, and pits, sagebrush, scorpions, poisonous snakes, and blinding, smothering silt beds. The most feared hazard of all, silt, is like talcum powder. It can be several feet deep with sharp ruts at the bottom. The silt cloud gets so thick, you just point the car, put your foot down, and hope."

In his autobiography, James Garner recalls driving Baja five or six times, beginning in 1968, and he did so in a wide variety of machinery, with numerous co-drivers. He also competed in other highly visible and important off-road events of the day, such as the Stardust 7-11 off-road Grand Prix and the Mint 400 in Nevada. NORRA, and its subsequent SCORE International off-road racing organization, have been sold and reorganized numerous times and the record keeping is a little murky, so Garner's complete off-road race log is difficult to assemble. However, by all accounts, he drove hard and smart, and acquitted himself well. Because of this, in 1978 he earned his rightful place as an inductee into the Off-Road Motorsports Hall of Fame.

Coincidentally, off-road racing legends and car builders Bill Stroppe and Vic Hickey were both born in 1919: Hickey in Akron, Ohio; Stroppe in Long Beach, California. It's no surprise they followed very different paths to greatness in terms of automotive engineering, innovation, and race car design and construction.

Stroppe began working at an automobile wrecking yard in Southern California, while still in high school, learning from the ground up how a car was put together (and taken apart). It wasn't long before this blossomed into an interest in high performance, and the building of race cars. Stroppe served in the U.S. Navy during World War II and earned a presidential citation for developing an innovative naval aircraft refueling system that tanked up airplanes aboard carriers in less time than previously. His business relationship with the Ford Motor Company began shortly after the end of the war.

The Vic Hickey–engineered and –built *Baja Boots* were duck-faced buggies with big GM V-8 engines mounted in back. The cars were innovative and fast but never lived up to their potential in terms of winning results. *Photo Courtesy Tom Madigan Archive*

Likely the world's most famous off-road racing Bronco, nicknamed *Big Oly* in recognition of its Olympia Beer sponsorship. This was the Stroppe-built machine that was finally tough enough to handle the abuse of Parnelli Jones, delivering multiple back-to-back Baja victories. Bill Stroppe himself often served as Jones' co-driver/navigator. *Photo Courtesy Tom Madigan Archive*

Stroppe was caught up with and active in the massive 1950s proliferation of hot rodding and racing, as well as building engines and cars for events as divergent as the Carrera Panamericana Mexican road race, and the Mobile [fuel] Economy Run program. He was involved with some very early NASCAR efforts, but the development that really lit his creative fire was the introduction of the Ford Bronco in 1965, and the birth of organized off-road racing that followed shortly thereafter.

Having experienced racing conditions in Mexico during the 1950s, Stroppe knew that the Bronco had the right stuff to be competitive in this new 1960s phenomenon called off-roading or "Baja" racing. He ultimately fielded entire teams of Broncos in the big off-road races (with James Garner and Scooter Patrick among the driver/co-driver pairings) and of course entered, built, co-drove, and navigated for Parnelli Jones in the famous *Big Oly* Bronco, which posted several overall Baja victories. In Ford and off-road racing circles, Stroppe is a legend.

James Garner and Bill Stroppe on the cover of *Off-Road* magazine's August 1972 issue. Garner's ride is the F-100 he shared with Slick Gardner, and Stroppe is with a compact Ford Courier truck, likely at this time a support vehicle, but these compact trucks were also developed as racers. *Photo Courtesy Tom Madigan Archive*

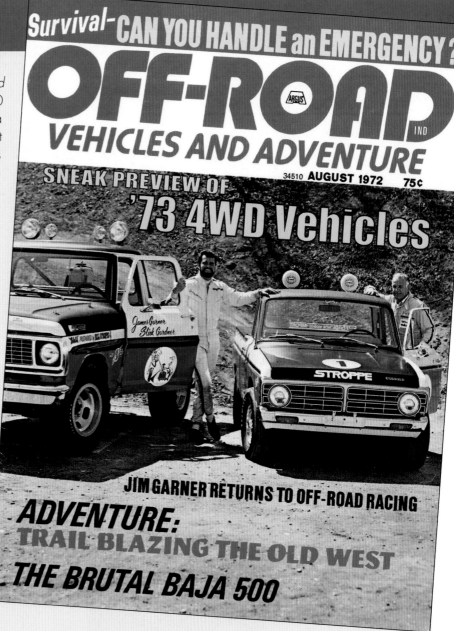

Vic Hickey also took an interest in all mechanized things at a young age, and when his family relocated from Ohio to Southern California, it put him square into the hotbed of the burgeoning hot rodding and racing scene. In the mid-1950s, he joined General Motors as an engineer; he designed, engineered, and built his own unique high-performance off-road vehicle called the Trailblazer.

You may recall that Chevrolet's first modern, truck-based off-roader/SUV of the late 1960s was called the Blazer; Hickey's "Trailblazer" name was revived in 2000 for use on another Chevrolet SUV. Hickey's most memorable off-road racing machine was called *Baja Boot*. It was a large, fast, rear-/mid-engined "buggy" powered by a General Motors V-8 engine. Steve McQueen and his friend/stunt double, race team member, and off-roading pioneer Bud Ekins raced one in Baja.

Hickey left General Motors in 1968 to form Hickey Enterprises, which designed and built a number of primarily off-road vehicles, parts, and accessories. As much as Bill Stroppe was a "Ford guy," Vic Hickey was a "GM guy" to the core. Even though James Garner began his off-road racing experience at Baja in Ford Broncos, he ultimately connected with Hickey, who was a key player in Garner's Oldsmobile sedan–based *Banshee* and *Grabber* racers.

Hickey also built several on-road GMC trucks that Garner drove and/or used in *The Rockford Files* (see Chapter Five).

Like Stroppe, Hickey is an automotive engineering and off-road racing legend; the two men, both now deceased, were longtime friends and competitors, and are members of the Off-Road Motorsports Hall of Fame.

The venue was a celebrity race at Riverside International Raceway in 1978; this is Garner smiling and hamming it up with actor/comedienne Ruth Buzzi of *Rowan & Martin's Laugh In* fame. All of the celebs piloted modified Jeep CJ-5s. Ms. Buzzi was obviously quite petite compared with the 6-foot 3-inch Garner, and she remains a committed automotive enthusiast. Garner appeared many times on *Laugh In*. *Photo Courtesy Tracksidephoto.com*

Parnelli Jones is famously quoted as saying that the Baja 1000 race is a 24-hour-long plane crash that never really ends, and here Mr. Garner looks like he's just been through one. Note the hand-lettered bottle marked Gatorade; not exactly official-looking factory packaging. *Photo Courtesy Willie Stroppe Collection*

The CJ-5s driven by the celebs in this event were lightly modified from street spec; major mods appear to be the removal of the factory folding-windshield structure and the addition of a roll cage protecting the entire passenger compartment. The addition of the Cibie driving lights seems an odd touch as the race took place during daylight hours. *Photo Courtesy Tracksidephoto.com*

James Garner, Slick Gardner, and their Andersen-sponsored, Stroppe-built F-100 at Baja in 1972 are shown in this image displayed at the Mendenhall Museum. Gardner commented that Garner "was no Parnelli Jones, but a pretty good driver, at least as good as most of the better guys running Baja at the time." Gardner recalls that once during the race, driver Garner put the car precipitously close to the edge of a ravine, and that the co-driver needed to reach over and yank the steering wheel to the right to avoid the truck taking a tumble. Being in the right seat is no easy place to be, with carsickness a common occurrence. Gardner recalls vomiting profusely once the team reached the finish line; his wife was concerned that he was having a heart attack. *Photo Courtesy Mendenhall Museum Collection*

This is Fred Phillips' unrestored and authentic A.I.R. Hurst SC/Rambler off-road racer. The cars were compact and fast; they ran with varying degrees of success. Some were rear-drive only, and a pair of them were built as four-wheel drivers. *Photo Courtesy Fred Phillips*

Until the mid-1960s, it was said that the only race that American Motors was interested in was the human race. However, as AMC's fortunes waned in the mid-1960s and it flirted with bankruptcy in 1967, the company made a 180-degree turnabout. The turnaround had already begun in 1966 with the introduction of its then-new 290-ci V-8. With the compact external dimensions of a typical small-block V-8, it was designed so that it could be expanded, first to 343, then 390, and ultimately 401 ci.

The big benefactor of the introduction of this modern V-8 was the compact Rambler American. Before 1966, AMC's existing 287/327 V-8s did not fit between the shock towers of AMC's American compact. This resulted in AMC's first response to the pony-car craze, the Marlin; it was built on the mid-sized Classic platform rather than the more logical compact American chassis.

Once AMC got more serious about performance, there was no turning back. With the introduction of the Javelin pony car in 1968 and the two-seat AMX six months later, AMC took the gloves off. AMC fielded a team in the Trans-Am series and before the midyear AMX introduction, AMC enlisted the help of Craig Breedlove to set 106 FIA-sanctioned long-distance speed records for its new AMX.

For 1969, in response to the number of low-buck, stripped-down, minimalist muscle cars, starting with Plymouth's 1968 Road Runner, AMC turned to Hurst for its answer, the AMC SC/Rambler. While mainstream Rambler Americans could be equipped with the 290 V-8, the 1,512 red, white, and blue SC/Ramblers were equipped with the dimensionally similar 390 (offered in the AMX) mated to a heavy-duty 4-speed manual transmission. For $2,995, anyone could walk into an AMC showroom and drive off in a car that would run a 14-second quarter-mile on street tires.

Fred Eltrich and Davey Jordan gunning their A.I.R. SC/Rambler through the Mexican desert in the first Baja 500. They were running well, among the race's front-runners, when a steering rod failed, causing a crash with a cactus. The drivers were unhurt but the car didn't fare so well; it did not finish. *A.I.R. Photo, Courtesy Davey Jordan Collection*

Apparently this was not lost on James Garner. His previous off-road racing involved some Holman-Moody-Stroppe–prepared Ford Broncos. However, when the necessary financial support didn't materialize from Ford, Garner teamed up with his friend, Riverside, California, millionaire John Crean, to put together an American International Racing (Garner's multiplatform racing team) off-road team for 1969. To publicize the team's efforts Crean turned to Los Angeles newspaperman William Springer, who connected the fledgling team with AMC brass.

After A.I.R. and AMC inked a three-year deal, Garner and Crean turned to Bill Rohrbacher, an experienced off-road racer with a well-equipped shop in Hemet, California, to build a team of 10 AMC SC/Rambler–based off-roaders. Eight of the cars were fairly conventional two-wheel-drive SC/Ramblers with the glass removed and with the wheel arches opened. Two were built with four-wheel drive, modified with a number of Jeep components.

The car shown here, owned by Fred Phillips of Calgary, Alberta, is one of those two four-wheel-drive SC/Ramblers, a true survivor purchased on eBay in about 2000 from the previous owner in Covina, California. What's interesting is that rather than restoring the ex–Garner/A.I.R. SC/Rambler to its past off-road glory, Phillips has elected to preserve the car as-is. It represents the car as it raced and is a true time capsule; it gives us a look at state-of-the-art off-road racing, circa 1969.

Rohrbacher's modifications to AMC's SC/Rambler included blueprinting the 390 V-8, which raised the output from 315 to 410 hp at the flywheel. With the installation of a 3.54:1 final drive, the two-wheel-drive off-road SC/Ramblers were capable of a top speed of 151 mph. Race-equipped with 4.11:1 gears, the cars were capable of "only" 132 mph, but with fearsome low-end acceleration. The Phillips car is reportedly the last car built and the only one of the 10 that was equipped with an automatic transmission, in this case a beefed-up Borg-Warner 3-speed. In addition to the Jeep suspension, four-wheel-drive components, transfer case, the cars were equipped with 44-gallon fuel cells.

Start to finish, all 10 cars were built within a 60-day period. Even with all the off-road modifications, they weighed within a few pounds of the SC/Rambler's factory 3,140-pound shipping weight.

The first race for the team was the 1969 Baja 500. AMC, through its *Redliner* house newsletter, provided the following recap.

Ensenada, Baja California, Mexico

An American Motors SC/Rambler from James Garner's American International Racing team won the PASSENGER CAR category June 11 to 12 in the Baja 500 Off-Road racing event, an automotive enduro race that stands as a challenge to both vehicle and driver.

A specially prepared team of bright red, white, and blue American Motors' sedans was entered in Category I and IV. Category I is open to production two-wheel-drive vehicles while Category IV is open to four-wheel-drive experimental vehicles.

This race is sanctioned by NORRA and is considered one of the toughest endurance races in the world, negotiating hundreds of miles of rocky, dusty terrain through the remote Baja (lower) California peninsula.

Veteran Grand Prix race driver Bob Bondurant of Santa Ana, California, with his co-driver, Tony Murphy of Los Angeles, California, roared across the finish line in an SC/Rambler after 19 hours and 5 minutes of racing around a treacherous 550-mile-long course that circles the upper half of the Baja California peninsula and returns to the finish line in the center of the resort city of Ensenada. "The performance of our SC/Rambler was truly remarkable," declared Bondurant. "We experienced no mechanical trouble despite the tremendous pounding our car took on the course."

Here is one of the retired A.I.R. SC/Rambler off-road racers wearing Chaffey College colors, and modified slightly from its A.I.R team days, with at least three wheels off the ground. This is one of the more-common 2WD machines; only two of the cars built had 4WD. Rancho Cucamonga, California's Chaffey College, had an automotive and auto racing technology program that was world renown. Many retired race cars were donated to the school over time, and many more were built by the students. *Photo Courtesy Karl Harmetz*

Class winners Bondurant and Murphy led three more A.I.R. SC/Ramblers home, gaining 3rd, and 5th place, as well as 13th place, in Class I. Finishing 3rd was Ed Orr of Studio City, California, and J. W. Wright of North Hollywood, California. In 5th place was Walker Evens of Riverside, California, and Don Simpson of Hemet, California, and 13th place was Dick Hansen of San Diego, California, and Johnnie Crean of Riverside, California.

In the Category IV class, adding to the impressive Bondurant/Murphy victory in Category I was Carl Jackson and Jim Fricker of Hemet, California, who finished in 4th place in

Bill Stroppe's letter, dated October 13, 1970, was brief and to the point, stating little more than that he was donating two "1969 Ramblers," making no mention of their history or racing provenance nor James Garner, to the school for "educational purposes." *Photo Courtesy Karl Harmetz*

Category IV, driving an experimental four-wheel-drive SC/ Rambler, the car that is now part of the Phillips collection.

Unfortunately the Baja 500 proved to be the high point of the A.I.R. program. While a few of the cars ran in that year's Baja 1000, the off-road team disbanded, apparently the victim of a falling out among the financial backers. The cars dispersed and this is the only known survivor.

The irony of the Jeep-infused Garner AMC SC/Ramblers is that they served as a precursor of what was to come. In 1970 AMC purchased the Jeep brand from Kaiser, setting the stage for its rapid expansion in the 1970s. The American-based SC/Rambler evolved into AMC's popular Hornet in 1970 and 10 years later AMC introduced the groundbreaking four-wheel-drive Eagle, ushering in, prematurely some will say, the era of the car-based crossover.

Thanks Jim.

Richard Truesdell

Garner appears suited up and ready to run in his No. 1 Jeep. Note that the "horse collar" is fully installed, and that his goggles are designed to fit close to the face to minimize dust in the eyes. Some drivers and co-drivers used the goggles with open-faced helmets, others with closed-faced helmets without the flip-up lenses closed or installed. *Photo Courtesy Tracksidephoto.com*

These are whimsical looks from many of Garner's more popular movie and TV characters. In some he might be Jim Rockford. In others he might be looking more like Jason McCullough, his leading role in *Support Your Local Sheriff!* Or maybe just charming, humorous, James Garner being himself, having a good "day at the races." Garner was 50 at this time, still playing Jim Rockford, still an immensely popular leading man in Hollywood, and seldom looked more handsome. *Photo Courtesy Tracksidephoto.com*

James Garner enjoyed reasonable success in the Baja races, never winning overall, but always finishing and notching several solid in-class results. In *The Garner Files* he says, "I finished the race every year, whether in a truck or a car, which is a testament to the people who built the vehicles, not the driver." That first effort, in 1968, sharing the Stroppe-built Ford Bronco with Scooter Patrick, resulted in a fourth-in-class finish. And at Baja, just surviving is a victory.

Garner admits that tackling Baja is tough racing . . . "and it's hard on the body, especially the back. Even though we'd worked on the suspensions to soften the bumps, at the end of a run I could barely stand up. Felt like I'd been gone over with a rubber hose, but the fun outweighed the pain."

In the Baja, you drive as fast as you can and hope your car doesn't break. He'd get up to 90 mph in the Bronco on those desert trails. "If you got stuck behind a slower car, you ran up, gave him a little bump in the back, and kept bumping him until he moved over. At night, you flashed your lights to signal a slower car in front of you to get out of the way. If you drove the Baja alone, you were in the car 15 to 20 hours in 100-degree heat during the day and subfreezing temperatures at night. The darkness complicated everything, of course."

The *Grabber* Racers

After running Baja in Broncos and an AMC sedan, James Garner began to explore the pioneering nature of Baja racing by attacking the race in a variety of Oldsmobile-based racing machines. He'd had a good run with Bill Stroppe in the Ford Broncos, and the AMCs built and entered by A.I.R. showed promise in the dirt. Nevertheless, he switched bandwagons, aligning himself with General Motors and legendary off-roading innovative engineer and car builder Vic Hickey to drive a stable of Oldsmobile 4-4-2– and Cutlass-bodied machines in the early 1970s.

They came in two flavors; first a pair called *Grabber*s (named after a line of Goodyear off-roading and truck tires) that ran conventional Olds V-8 engines up front, powering the rear wheels, followed by a truly wild child, *Banshee*, which put the engine right where the front passenger seat normally was.

During the 1960s, sports car racing had morphed from primarily front-engined race cars to those with the engine in the middle, just aft of the driver, for better overall weight balance. However, this notion was truly otherworldly for off-roading. Most of the racers were front-engine cars or trucks of one stripe or another; a variety were rear-engined, primarily Volkswagen-powered sand rails, buggies, and "Baja bugs." Vic Hickey changed all that.

The first *Grabber* that Garner drove at Baja wore pre-production 1970 bodywork even though he ran it in the 1969 Baja 1000. Even though the car wore 4-4-2 badges, it was more technically a high-performance W-31 Cutlass by virtue of its 350-ci Olds V-8, instead of a 4-4-2's 455-ci big-block. Regardless, the W-31 spooled out more than 300 hp, absolutely enough, to be competitive in the race.

> "If you got stuck behind a slower car, you ran up, gave him a little bump in the back, and kept bumping him until he moved over."

So much of what made the Oldsmobile *Banshee* and *Grabbers* successful was the ground clearance that Vic Hickey engineered into the design. Sedan-bodied racers usually leave too many components exposed underneath in spite of builders' best efforts to cover them with skidplates and such. So cranking up the ride height mitigated the problem to a great degree.

Equally important, and well illustrated here, is the widely cut out and radiused wheel openings to allow for the tall and wide off-road tires. When running competitive speeds, these cars flew several feet through the air over heaves and bumps, landing hard, and the suspension needed lots of travel to handle the punishment. Long-travel suspensions and shocks, widely radiused wheel openings, and lots of ground clearance worked to keep the cars from breaking apart, and from needlessly punishing the drivers. This car had already been converted to run 1969 Olds bodywork and huge, dual fuel fillers on the rear sail panels. *Photo Courtesy Tracksidephoto.com*

The car was based on stock underpinnings, substantially reinforced with 1/8-inch steel plate welded all over the factory GM chassis. The suspension was also beefed up considerably, running dual sets of Delco shocks at each wheel. The ride height was raised several inches, the wheel wells were modified to contain the huge Goodyear racing tires, and the car ran larger, GM, steel truck wheels painted body color.

The front headlights were swapped out for brighter, aircraft landing light–quality sealed beams. Ancillary night driving lights were mounted on the roof.

The standard fuel tank was swapped out for a proper racing fuel cell, and the interior was also stripped out, racing style. A full NASCAR-spec roll cage was welded into the cabin for driver protection as well as additional chassis rigidity and structural strength. A factory-style short center console (including a cigarette lighter!) was retained between the front bucket seats, which also housed the Hurst Dual-Gate shifter for the Turbo 400 automatic transmission.

Ultimately, two *Grabbers* were built. This one is now painted white and is virtually identical to the car James Garner raced. The Mendenhall family of Buellton, California, owns it. Note the four night-racing landing lights mounted on the roof, and masses of duct tape holding things together aft of the co-driver's seat. This is the result of a long, hard life of off-road racing. You can be sure that Vic Hickey didn't originally engineer the car to be held together with duct tape. *Photo Courtesy Mel Stone*

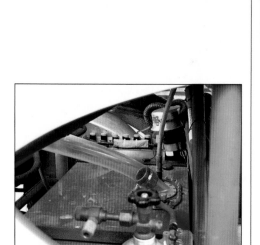

This is the *Banshee's* fuel cell, mounted just aft of the engine, in what would normally be the car's rear passenger-seat area. Note the heavily padded roll bar just in front of it. *Photo Courtesy Mel Stone*

The factory instrument panel was completely removed; it was replaced by a fabricated aluminum flat-panel dash to house a full complement of Stewart Warner gauges, and all of the ancillary switchgear to operate the lights and various systems. A Motorola FM radio was mounted on the far right of the dash for use by the co-driver/navigator to keep in contact with the team base. A large aluminum multi-stage air filtration canister filled up most of the passenger footwell. The engine and transmission were protected by large heavy-duty steel skidplates.

The 350-inch Olds was left largely stock except for the wide-open racing exhaust system, the sophisticated air filtration unit, multiple fuel filters installed at various points in the fuel lines, and the addition of a pair of heavy-duty A/C electric fuel pumps. The rear-end ratio was 3.90:1, giving the car extra low-end grunt and compensating for the torque effect lost to the extra-tall Goodyear Pikes Peak tires that ran liner tubes front and rear. The Olds came from the factory with disc brakes up front, but they were also installed in the rear. The factory bucket seats were replaced with Safety Racing Buckets from Steve McQueen's Solar Plastics company.

There was no official indication of any factory support from General Motors, but although Vic Hickey had long since retired from General Motors, the hush talk was that Hickey received more than a little engineering assistance from General Motors in building the car. It wasn't the last time.

When the vibrant blue and yellow 4-4-2 was unloaded from the trucks in Baja in preparation for the mandatory technical and safety inspection, not everyone was convinced that the big stock-bodied coupe was the right answer or much of a clear path to

Most off-road builders used aircraft landing lights to light up the night through the dark Mexican desert during the long 1,000-mile races, which typically took up to 30 hours to complete. *Photo Courtesy Mel Stone*

James Garner with the Mendenhall *Grabber*. Some years after Garner stopped racing the Oldsmobile off-roaders, he paid a visit to the Mendenhall family, who had since acquired one of the *Grabbers*. It was originally blue and yellow but has since been painted white and wears local sponsorship from businesses near Jack Mendenhall's Buellton-area home and business. Mendenhall was active in off-road racing from 1968 to 1974, racing this ex–Hickey/Garner Olds from 1972 to 1974. Vic Hickey's race shop, where the cars were built, wasn't far away. *Photo Courtesy Mendenhall Museum Collection*

WARNING
.SANDY DESERT ROAD.
HAVE AMPLE SUPPLIES
OF GAS - OIL & WATER

The Mendenhall *Grabber*, rebodied with 1969 model-year Olds bodywork, hasn't been run in a decade, but is largely original and remains much the same as when as Mark's father, Jack, raced the car some years ago. The Andersen sponsorship is the world-famous Andersen's Split Pea Soup restaurant in Buellton, about a mile from the Mendenhall's original shop, gas station, and current petroliana and racing museum collection. *Photo Courtesy Mel Stone*

victory in Baja. However, they had already seen that James Garner was up to the task as an off-road racer, and his co-driver/navigator Don Mauer, an experienced right-seater and solid racing mechanic, was a superb teammate to have along. And nobody ever wrote off a Hickey-designed and -built car before a race, no matter how unconventional.

James Garner talks of the race and results in the March 1970 issue of *Popular Hot Rodding* magazine; Garner and *Grabber* also appeared on the cover. Editor Lee Kelley reported, "Garner and Mauer stormed down the Mexican peninsula in 26 hours and 24 minutes, finishing in second place in their class, a mere 34 minutes behind the winning Saab." Keep in mind that anything less than 30 hours was considered an extremely fast time to complete the Baja's 1000, so the boys were really pounding the dirt in the big blue Olds.

Kelley continues: "So what did Garner have to say about his strong second-place finish?" 'We should have won the race; it's my fault that we didn't. We had a lead of 1½ hours over the Saab at La Purisima (the seventh checkpoint), so we decided to stroke it [go easy] over the last stretch of rough stuff into Villa Constitucion (the eighth and final checkpoint) and then really wail once we got on the pavement into La Paz. Because of the [piston ring] setup we were using in the engine, we pumped out quite a bit of oil between those two checkpoints, and because we didn't refuel at Constitucion we didn't make an oil check. When we got onto the pavement we could only run about 30 mph; anything faster and the oil pressure would fall below 20 pounds. By the time we found some oil (in a little Mexican Café) we were behind again. But I guess we showed them that our "big old Olds" was competitive, didn't we?'" Yes, you did.

Ultimately two *Grabber*s were built, one wearing 1969 Olds Cutlass bodywork, and they lived on for many years, past their tenure in the Hickey racing stable, as active off-road racing competitors. The Mendenhall family of Buellton, California, now owns one of them; the other, the actual car raced by James Garner, ended up damaged, rusted,

Jack Mendenhall worked at a garage/wrecking yard in Buellton. At some point he swapped the original GM steel wheels for these lighter, MotorWheel alloys. *Photo Courtesy Mel Stone*

Garner powers his Hickey-built Olds *Grabber* through Baja. Hayden's oil and transmission coolers was the car's major sponsor for this run, and Baja's tormenting conditions certainly put the hardware to the test. These cars performed credibly in the Baja 1000, giving Garner a hard-earned class win. *Photo Courtesy Tracksidephoto.com*

Note the use of a roof-mounted spoiler, because believe it or not, aerodynamics was pretty important on these high-riding off-road racers. Speeds of well over 100 mph on long straight stretches were possible, and because the cars rode so high, airflow under the chassis often caused unwanted lift. *Photo Courtesy Mel Stone*

This is an interesting collection of snapshots taken at the Hickey Enterprises shop during the *Banshee*'s construction. Note the fender liners mounted to the chassis, not to the removable bodywork. Not many people believe how exotic and sophisticated purpose-built off-roaders like this could be. Note the dual fuel-feed tubes to help facilitate quicker pit stops, and the super-heavy-duty control arms used up front to help stand the gaff of the car flying through the air; plus two-per-side shock absorber mounts. *Photo Courtesy Mendenhall Museum Collection*

sans powertrain, and somewhat abandoned. It was recently acquired by Ron Johnson of Tacoma, Washington, and treated to a comprehensive restoration. It has since competed in the reborn NORRA vintage off-road racing 250, and is featured in the March 2011 edition of *Hot Rod* magazine.

One particularly interesting occurrence during the 1970 running of the Baja 500 involved Garner, co-driver/navigator Doug Roe, and one of the *Grabbers*. Garner and Roe were pounding through the desert and broke a tie-rod that rendered the car unsteerable. They didn't have a replacement part onboard, but didn't want to sit in the desert and wait for rescue, so they made do with what they had. They splinted and bandaged the damaged suspension piece mostly together with wrenches, tape, and wire, and continued on. The resulting pit repair took nearly seven hours, and the Garner/Roe *Grabber* finished a decidedly off-pace 14th overall.

The Oldsmobile *Banshee*

If you thought the notion of racing a stock-bodied Olds Cutlass at Baja was a stretch, just check out *Banshee*.

James Garner tells the genesis of its story in his autobiography: "Vic Hickey, a senior engineer at General Motors, designed the Oldsmobile *Banshee* in 1972 . . . I was interested

Banshee was as "one of a kind" as an off-road racer could be, and wore an odd mix of badging, with 442 emblems on the nosepiece and Cutlass badges on the side. It mattered little, as *Banshee* was a "Funny Car" in the purest sense, with a scaled-down fiberglass body over a stout tubular-steel chassis. *Photo Courtesy Mel Stone*

Banshee pays a visit to the Mendenhall's petroliana and racing museum in Buellton, where it used to live. This wonderful place is filled with an amazing collection of gas pumps, pump globes, oil cans, bottles, vintage photos, tools, neon signs, vintage race cars, and more. Group visits can be arranged via mendenhallmuseum.com. *Photo Courtesy Mel Stone*

Vic Hickey's considerable contribution to *Banshee* is acknowledged only in this modest lettering. This is no great surprise since Hickey was a very humble man, often minimizing talk of his own genius and contribution to any successful project. He ultimately marketed a successful line of Chevrolet and GMC off-road racing and truck parts, and he built several GMC trucks driven by James Garner that were also used in his television show, *The Rockford Files*. *Photo Courtesy Mel Stone*

Note the complete lack of a rear window, the norm for off-road racers. The huge fuel-filler neck connects to a large fuel cell mounted just aft of the engine and driver's seat. *Photo Courtesy Mel Stone*

in the development of the car, so I would drop in on the weekends while it was being built. I'd remembered that a Formula One car has the engine positioned toward the rear instead of in front, to prevent the weight from making the car nose down when it went airborne after hitting a bump. Therefore, we put the *Banshee*'s engine next to the driver.

"With all that weight in the right-center, and my [the driver's] weight on the left-center to balance it out, *Banshee* flew straight and landed flat, a big advantage in both handling and safety. *Banshee* was unique for its time. It looked like an Olds Cutlass, but shorter and wider. It has a 500-hp aluminum-block engine to give it a little more power."

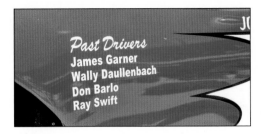

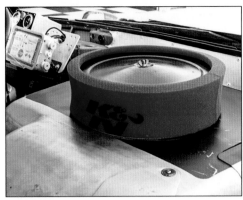

Just a few of the *Banshee's* many noteworthy pilots are listed here; note the misspelling of Wally Dallenbach's last name. Wally Dallenbach, Sr., enjoyed a long and fruitful Indy car-racing career during the USAC Champ–Car series days, and ultimately served as an IRL race official. Ray Swift owned *Banshee* after Hickey stopped racing it. He then sold the car to the Mendenhall family, and son Jon Swift has since repurchased the car and still runs it in vintage off-road events. *Photo Courtesy Mel Stone*

You might not ordinarily expect to see an air filter where there ought to be a passenger seat, but it makes sense in *Banshee* because the engine is mounted where a front-seat passenger would ordinarily sit. The engine cover is fashioned out of aluminum, and opens via Dzus quick-release fasteners. *Photo Courtesy Mel Stone*

Banshee uses a Pontiac GTO hood tach so the driver can keep his eyes up and on the road while continuing to monitor engine revs. Inside the car, the instrumentation is relatively spare, with the view dominated by the scrolling navigation device. Why would Hickey have to use a Pontiac piece on an Olds? Simple enough: Oldsmobile never offered a hood-mounted tach on the 4-4-2. *Photo Courtesy Mel Stone*

Banshee is a single-seat race car because of its mid-engined layout, thus there's no co-driver/navigator to help guide the driver through the desert. Instead, *Banshee* runs this scrolling navigational device that rolls the driving notes "toilet-roll style," an interesting precursor to today's sophisticated GPS navigation systems. *Photo Courtesy Mel Stone*

This low, wide shot gives some perspective on the *Banshee* short wheelbase and well-muscled persona. Suspension travel is a generous 12 or so inches (generous back then), allowing room for the large off-road tires to travel up and down in the widely radiused fenderwell openings. *Photo Courtesy Mel Stone*

The *Banshee* fiberglass visage is fairly accurate in representing a 1969 4-4-2, although the hood more resembles the 1970–1972 Olds ram-air piece. *Photo Courtesy Mel Stone*

Even though *Banshee* resembles a semi-stock 1969 Olds Cutlass, its scale plays tricks on the eye. Current owner Jon Swift estimates it to be about a 2/3-scale version of the car on which it is based, but there's very little factory Oldsmobile architecture underneath. In that sense, *Banshee* is much like a Funny Car drag racer, a bit of a caricature body on a purpose-built, all-racing, tubular chassis. In addition, the car's geography was all rethought by Hickey, no stranger to building mid-engined machinery for off-road racing. His legendary *Baja Boot* raced in the first Mexican 1000 of 1967, and then for several more years after that. It mounted a small-block Chevy V-8 just aft of the passenger compartment.

Banshee was designed from scratch, around a fully independent suspension (three shocks at each corner) and boasted an impressive suspension and wheel travel for the time: 8 to 12 inches. Today's top-level off-road racers measure suspension travel in terms of feet, using shock absorbers with separate oil tanks and their own cooling system. But a foot of travel was a lot in 1972. The engine sat where the passenger seat normally was, so *Banshee* was obviously a single-seat racer with no room for a co-driver/navigator. The automatic transmission runs backward to a live rear axle. The Hurst shifter sits just to the left of the engine, at the driver's right hand.

Up front, where you'd normally expect to find the engine, are radiators and oil coolers. The slightly shrink-wrapped bodywork is made of fiberglass, and the headlights are mounted to the frame, not to the grille or bodywork. The car's hood scoops do not function to tunnel intake air into the carburetor, but instead to channel a bit more cooling air to the dual radiators and ancillary coolers. Pure race stuff, pure Hickey genius.

The aluminum-block 455-ci V-8 powering *Banshee* is a very rare and special engine indeed. The alloy-block 455 was initially developed for drag racing, but Hickey's considerable ties to GM racing departments put one at his disposal. The engine was by nature more powerful than a production, cast-iron version, but it was much lighter; it was said to be around 150 pounds trimmer than an iron 455. That's a meaningful weight reduction in a race car, and *Banshee* wasn't exactly a flyweight considering its heavy tubular steel frame, steel wheels, steel suspension components, multiple shock absorbers, and such, although its scaled-down size and fiberglass body surely made it lighter than a stock-bodied and stock-chassied 442 of the same era.

In a somewhat charming bit of hot rodding, and GM corporate branding, *Banshee* wore stock Oldsmobile bottle cap–style hubcaps on its massive steel wheels, and ran specially treaded and compounded tires loosely patterned after those used on heavy equipment and farm implements. Transmission coolers and the fuel cell were mounted just about where the passenger seat is in a conventionally bodied Cutlass.

Journalist/photographer Nina Padgett wrote about *Banshee* in the January 22, 1996, issue of *Autoweek* magazine, quoting carbuilder Hickey as praising James Garner's off-road driving prowess. "While he wasn't the world's most fearless driver, he had the best retention of any man who drove for me. On a pre-run, if he hit a bump, he'd come back five days later and tell you where it was within 10 feet.

The same story outlines the car's competition record. "Garner only won one race in *Banshee*. That was the Riverside Grand Prix, run along a riverbed near Riverside,

Slick Gardner, Mark Mendenhall, and Jon Swift (left to right) have been off-road racing with and against each other for many years, and have bought, sold, and traded cars among themselves as well. All are from multi-generational racing families, and have owned and driven a variety of ex–James Garner off-road racing cars and trucks. This is what *Banshee* looks like today, at Mendenhall's racing and petroliana museum. *Photo Courtesy Mel Stone*

This high-angle view gives a better look at how much shorter and squatter *Banshee* is than a conventional production-bodied 1969 4-4-2. It also shows that the original body-colored steel wheels have given way to more modern alloy wheels. *Photo Courtesy Mel Stone*

California. He usually ran near the front of the pack, and often placed high in the final standings. Oddly, his only competition accident in *Banshee* came in the race he won.

"According to Hickey, Garner momentarily took his eyes off the course near the finish at Riverside, and flipped *Banshee* into the river. Garner crawled out and threw his helmet in the mud in disgust. Yet he was so far ahead that he was eventually declared the winner.

"The actor had one other wreck in *Banshee*; it was a big one, in an early shakedown, when the car was going at least two-thirds of its 144-mph top speed. He went into a corner at about a hundred miles an hour, lost it in the sand, and flipped the car about five times."

James Garner tells the same stories as follows: "*Banshee* placed high in a few races and won the Riverside Grand Prix, even though I hit the sand and had to jump the car into a mud pond near the start/finish. I was so disgusted with myself; I jumped out of the car and smashed my helmet on the ground (the crowd loved that). I also rolled it a few times in a practice run but it was strong enough to protect me."

Several other off-roading greats also ran *Banshee*, including the late Mickey Thompson, a highly innovative race car designer/builder, although he never won in the bullish blue Olds.

It was raced at least once by Indy car great Wally Dallenbach, and then was owned and also raced by the father and son team of Jack and Mark Mendenhall from Buellton, California. Bud Ekins also raced *Banshee*. Central California enthusiast and racer Jon Swift currently owns the car.

The Mendenhall museum is filled with framed photos, magazine articles, and newspaper clippings about the histories of the Swift, Mendenhall, and Gardner family drivers and racing exploits. This *Tri-County Sportsman* clip shows a pair of the Oldsmobile racers, plus James Garner and Slick Gardner. *Photo Courtesy Mel Stone*

Jack Mendenhall's original open-face helmet still sits quietly in *Grabber*. The car has not been driven for some years, and remains very much as Mark Mendenhall's late father last raced it. *Photo Courtesy Mel Stone*

While strolling through the museum, you will find this interesting display. *Banshee* could fly through the air with the greatest of ease, especially since the engine and transmission were mounted amidships, right where the passenger seat would normally be.

Indy car driver Wally Dallenbach was at the controls for this wheelstand shot, and the poster is displayed casually at the Mendenhall garage and racing museum. Note the oil bottle, business card holder, old framed photo, and pair of pliers holding the edges of the photo onto a coffee table. *Photo Courtesy Mel Stone*

The Garner/Gardner F-100 prepares to take the start at Baja. The street in Ensenada is lined with hundreds of spectators. Back then, they were not restrained in any way or fenced off from the column of cars that take off down the street at full throttle. Many viewers attempt to reach out and touch the car as it goes by; one of Baja's many charming, if not dangerous, cultural aspects. *Photo Courtesy Tom Madigan Archive*

James Garner again partnered with his frequent teammate and co-driver Scooter Patrick to run this Porsche-powered Meyers Manx buggy at the Stardust 7-11 off-road race in Nevada in 1968. The buggy was fast but did not finish. The fenders appear to have been cut away after the drivers' names were painted on the front deck, and a large aluminum fuel tank has been grafted to the driver's side of the buggy. *Photo Courtesy Tom Madigan Archive*

This iconic shot shows the Hickey Enterprises Oldsmobile family tree: Garner's 1970 *Grabber* 4-4-2 at the left, the Mendenhall *Grabber* in the center (now painted white), and the one-and-only *Banshee* at the right. *Photo Courtesy Tom Madigan Archive*

James Garner is a very proud American; he wanted to make that very clear with the naming of his racing team and the choice of red, white, and blue as the team colors. International meant that they intended to compete on an international level against the best from anywhere in the world. They did, at major international-level endurance races, such as Sebring and Daytona. *Photo Courtesy Richard Prince*

A.I.R. *American International Racing Team*

" Making *Grand Prix* gave me the racing bug. After soaking up the atmosphere on the Formula One circuit and driving fast cars on racetracks all over Europe, I had to be involved in the sport.

— *James Garner* "

J ames Garner, much like Roger Penske, realized that racing could be a business, operated for fun, accomplishment, and profit; it could be organized and operated in a businesslike manner, with the intent of providing marketing and entertainment opportunities to a variety of businesses. This, and his recently ignited passion for professional-level motorsport, was the genesis of American International Racing (A.I.R.).

Chapter Four

Garner wasn't alone in this venture, forming his multi-tiered racing organization with a small group of well-qualified partners: Donald Rabbitt, long involved in motorsports PR and promotions; Dick Guldstrand, the seminal Corvette racer and expert at race car prep and construction; Irwin Sandin; and Bob Bondurant. Their idea was to compete in a variety of professional racing series, with an eye toward being successful in several of those platforms, and offering sponsors and marketing partners the opportunity to choose which most suited their business and marketing needs and models. Goodyear Tire & Rubber Company was one of A.I.R.'s founding sponsors.

The Plan

A.I.R.'s ambitions were aggressive, with plans to field teams in several different racing series simultaneously. These included sports car and endurance racing (focusing primarily on the big, well-known long-distance races such as the 12 Hours of Sebring and the 24 Hours of Daytona), Formula A (American racing similar to Formula One, using similar open-wheeled chassis and primarily American, naturally aspirated V-8 engines), and off-road. Formula A ultimately became the popular SCCA Formula 5000 series.

James Garner makes a point to Dick Guldstrand (left) and Chevrolet salesman Bob Wingate (middle) at the A.I.R. shop in 1968. Both team Corvettes are visible. *A.I.R. Photo, Courtesy Davey Jordan Collection*

Garner meets with unidentified guests at the A.I.R. Culver City shop. Note Garner's Goodyear racing jacket, as the tire company was a major sponsor, equipment provider, and source of funding for the team. Parts of two of the team's Corvettes are visible. Note Garner's signature in the lower right of this photo. *A.I.R. Photo, Courtesy Davey Jordan Collection*

The team set up a 6,000-square-foot facility in Southern California's famous "Thunder Alley" area of Culver City, where Guldstrand already had a shop. They were also close to Traco, the famous racing engine builder, which built and modified the team's racing Chevrolet V-8s.

James Garner said in a 1968 team press release, "American International Racing actually began many months ago during a discussion about sponsors in racing; why so many have come and so few remained. Amazingly, we all felt the same about the sponsors' plight, historically, in racing: They really hadn't gotten their money's worth. The reason for this dilemma, in our opinions, is two-fold: First, many sponsors are not fully aware of the values of racing and how to apply them; and second, most racers are totally concerned with building and fielding an automobile . . . forgetting the reasons why the sponsor invested in them in the first place."

As Garner promised, A.I.R. was structured with a "twin platoon" mentality: One group of people concentrated on building and running the cars, another focused on sponsor management and support. He continued, "American International Racing's aim is not only to be a success in business, but, we hope, to be able to lend a hand in whatever way possible to the future development and growth of our great sport."

In spite of his considerable ability as a racing driver, Garner made it clear from the beginning that his role as team owner and director would be administered from the pit lane and front office, not behind the wheel.

The Corvettes and the Drivers in 1968

A.I.R. was officially formed in July 1967; the first prong of its multi-faceted attack on motorsport was to be a two-car assault on the big-bore Grand Touring (GT) class at the 24 Hours of Daytona in 1968. To that end, the team purchased three new 1968 L-88 model Corvettes: Chevrolet's 427-ci thinly disguised racing Corvette.

These required very little major modification to hit the track; indeed the spirit of the GT classes was that cars be production-based and allowed very little architectural deviation from their stock configuration. GT-class cars needed to run the factory chassis and most of the street bodywork, an admittedly high-performance version of a factory-offered powertrain, and little in the way of exotic suspension or aerodynamic aid. A.I.R. vice president (and driver) Dick Guldstrand and chief mechanic Robert McDonald were in charge of preparing the cars for competition.

The idea behind purchasing three Corvettes was that two would be designated and prepped as the team's pure racing cars, while the third car would be a bit of a "public relations" car used for shows, dealer visits, and sponsor support activities.

The third car (the fabulous blue machine featured in many photos in this chapter) was available in case certain parts were needed, or to be pressed into competition duty at the last minute (only if absolutely necessary), which never happened.

First-rank, big-name sports car racers, such as Mario Andretti, Mark Donohue, the

> To that end, the team purchased three new 1968 L-88 model Corvettes: Chevrolet's 427-ci thinly disguised racing Corvette.

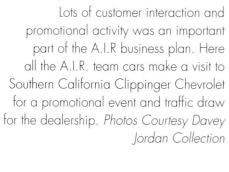

Lots of customer interaction and promotional activity was an important part of the A.I.R business plan. Here all the A.I.R. team cars make a visit to Southern California Clippinger Chevrolet for a promotional event and traffic draw for the dealership. *Photos Courtesy Davey Jordan Collection*

One of the great "Corvettemeisters" of all time, Dick Guldstrand was an A.I.R. team principal and driver. Guldstrand, nicknamed "Goldie," raced for Roger Penske in his earliest days as a racing team owner, nearly always in Corvettes. Guldstrand has built or driven many of the world's most notable racing Corvettes, and even designed and marketed his own special-edition model, the Guldstrand GS90. He still owns and operates a shop dedicated to modifying, maintaining, and race-prepping Corvettes and GM muscle cars. *A.I.R. Photo, Courtesy Davey Jordan Collection*

Unser brothers, A. J. Foyt, and many others, were beyond the reach and budget of the A.I.R. team, but Garner and company assembled a suitable, and highly respected, team of independent road racers. They included experienced Corvette pilot and team principle Dick Guldstrand along with fast and ultra-versatile Merlin "Scooter" Patrick (with whom Garner had teamed in the Baja 1000).

Patrick was an inspired choice not only because Garner knew him and they had worked together under intense racing conditions, but as a former mechanic and shop owner, Patrick understood the mechanical sensitivities of racing cars and car setup. He'd begun racing in 1959, and although until joining A.I.R. much of his race log was recorded at the wheel of Porsches, he was a superbly versatile and flexible driver and could easily adapt to the wide variety of machinery that A.I.R planned to compete with. After the A.I.R., Patrick went on to enjoy a successful career in sports cars and in the SCCA Can-Am series.

Known and brought aboard primarily for his success in racing Corvettes, Herb Caplan didn't return to run the team's Lolas after the L-88 program wound down. *A.I.R. Photo, Courtesy Davey Jordan Collection*

Mr. Versatile, the always-focused, always-fast Merlin "Scooter" Patrick. He raced the Corvettes, Lolas, and Formula A car, and also co-drove and navigated with James Garner in several off-road races. Patrick was also an accomplished Porsche racer, and competed in the SCCA Can-Am series as well. *A.I.R. PR Photo, Courtesy Davey Jordan Collection*

James Garner called him one of the coolest cats he's ever known; another superb all-rounder, Davey Jordan. *A.I.R. Photo, Courtesy Davey Jordan Collection*

The late Ed Leslie not only enjoyed an impressive career as a racing driver, but was also a decorated Army Air Corps pilot, who flew numerous important missions during World War II. According to his 2005 obituary in the *Monterey Herald* newspaper, Leslie was reassigned to the Military Air Transport service. He spent until 1947 ferrying DC-3s to Russia; B-24s and B-25s to New Guinea, Hawaii, Tarawa, and Guadalcanal; and DC-4s to Manila, Guam, Okinawa, and Tokyo. Due to his 1,550 hours of flight time, he was selected to fly for General Curtis LeMay in the U.S.A.F. Strategic Air Command, and served another three years amassing another 1,300 hours, including 30 bombing missions. He was awarded the Distinguished Flying Cross for Bravery. *A.I.R. Photo, Courtesy Davey Jordan Collection*

A.I.R. was indeed a team effort. Here's much of the gang, posing with one of the racing Corvettes outside the Culver City race shop. This photo has also been autographed and personalized by James Garner. *A.I.R. Photo, Courtesy Davey Jordan Collection*

The supremely competent Davey Jordan, who, like Patrick, was initially best known as a Porsche racer, had a deep racing resume in a variety of marques and series, beginning in the late 1950s. After leaving the A.I.R., Jordan continued racing 5.0-liter open-wheel Formula A and Can-Am.

Herb Caplan was a well-known West Coast amateur sports car racer and SCCA champion, particularly successful in Corvettes. He was an obvious choice to join the A.I.R. Corvette squad for Daytona in 1968.

Journeyman all-arounder Ed Leslie was also a distinguished, decorated World War II fighter pilot. All of the drivers had cool heads, knew how to go fast in a wide variety of machinery, could protect an ailing race car, and could work together as a cohesive team.

The L-88 was a serious muscle car, and Guldstrand and the team modified it as much as possible, within the competition rules, to make it much faster and up to the task of 24 hours of endurance racing punishment. All three Le Mans Blue Corvettes were roadster-bodied pre-production L-88s with early renditions of the high-performance aluminum "open chamber" cylinder heads atop their 427-ci blocks. The cars were built with many of the high-performance options they would need for competition use, including massive Holley carburetors, Muncie M-22 4-speed manual transmissions, and upgraded brakes and cooling. Of course they did without all the street accouterments that weren't necessary: no air conditioning, of course, no power windows, no audio systems, and no convertible tops.

At the Guldstrand/A.I.R. shop, the factory steel wheels were replaced with forged magnesium American Racing alloys and Goodyear racing tires. The already minimalist interiors were stripped; roll cages, racing exhaust, and fire systems were added; and they received everything else that went along with converting a high-performance street muscle sports car to endurance racing GT class specs.

The driver lineups were Guldstrand/Leslie/Caplan in the No. 44 machine; Patrick/Jordan teamed in the No. 45 car. In spite of having only rolled off of the GM assembly line in late November, the cars were fast when it was time to qualify for the early-February

The A.I.R. Corvettes qualified first and second in the GT class. This amateur snapshot shows them next to each other on the 1968 Daytona starting grid. Speed wasn't their problem, reliability was. *A.I.R. Photo, Courtesy Davey Jordan Collection*

It's a long road to Daytona, especially from Southern California. Here's one of the team cars on the road in 1968. It's interesting to see how the "art of the race team tow vehicle" has evolved over the years. Garner's team obviously kept it simple, whereas some of the more flamboyant drag racing and Indy car teams of the day had elaborate if not luxurious semi tractor/trailer rigs that would hold several cars, and a stockpile of parts, often served as team lodging or hospitality bases as well.

Mario Andretti once told me that the parking lot at the USAC Champ Car races was often filled with "station wagons towing single-car open trailers, with a few gas cans and some spare tires." *A.I.R. Photo, Courtesy Davey Jordan Collection*

1968 Daytona enduro, outrunning all the other GT category players. They qualified first and second in class: impressive.

Race Results

Hopes were high for the race, but the result was unfortunately low. In his autobiography, James Garner summarized his feelings about his team's Corvette program. "Big mistake. They were so unreliable; we raced them only once, at Daytona in 1968. We sold them and moved up to Formula A." They ultimately secured a matched pair of year-old Lola T70s for the longer endurance races.

In spite of solid preparation, superb drivers, and the impressive qualifying performance, the cars didn't fare well in the long hard race.

Jordan was aboard the No. 45 car, in the GT class lead, when a head bolt worked its way loose, causing a massive coolant leak, a blown head gasket, and terminal engine overheating; day done and a DNF for the Jordan/Patrick A.I.R. Corvette. The No. 44 car fared

The A.I.R. Corvettes are running together through the Daytona infield road course during practice. The Daytona International Speedway is a classic "Roval" course, employing portions of the high-banked turns used for the Daytona 500 and other NASCAR events, plus a multiple-turn road-racing configuration cut into the track's expansive infield. Daytona's 1968 configuration for the 24-hour race was 3.81 miles long, with the overall winning Porsche 907 covering 673 laps for 2,564.13 miles. *A.I.R. Photo, Courtesy Davey Jordan Collection*

Mr. Cool aboard his A.I.R. Corvette at Daytona, 1968. As an endurance racer, Davey Jordan had it all: a cool head, plenty of speed when he needed to turn it on, and a mechanical sensitivity that allowed him to get the most out of a strong-running car, or nurse an ailing machine to the finish. And as you'd expect of an "old-school gentleman" he still addresses his former team owner as "Mr. Garner." *A.I.R. Photo, Courtesy Davey Jordan Collection*

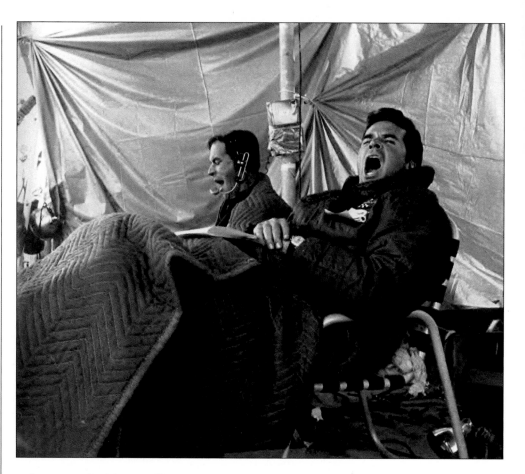

"

In spite of solid preparation, superb drivers, and the impressive qualifying performance, the cars didn't fare well in the long, hard race.

"

only marginally better, suffering a variety of mechanical maladies along the way, including lots of lost time for replacing numerous overheating rear differentials.

Mercifully, after 24 very long hours of grinding its way around the Daytona road course, the Guldstrand/Leslie/Caplan A.I.R. Corvette was credited with an unclassified finish, due to not having completed enough laps. Unofficially, it ranked 29th in class, several dozen laps down to the GT winner.

It wasn't long before Bondurant departed his position in A.I.R., having long wanted to launch his own high-performance driving and racing school. Bondurant left on good terms with his partners, remaining friends with James Garner to this day. Bondurant adds, "I could see that we all had different agendas, and I really just wanted to open my school." Of course, he did open the school and it has since become one of the best-known and most-respected high-performance driving programs in the world.

As Garner mentioned earlier, the two Corvette race cars were sold to other racing teams. Each enjoyed a relatively fruitful post-A.I.R. competition career; they occasionally show up on the vintage racing circuit.

Works in progress: A.I.R.'s trio of L-88 Corvettes at the A.I.R./Guldstrand shop. The promo/PR car is likely the one in the foreground, as it does not have the side pipes worn by the actual race cars. Note James Garner's autograph at the top of this photo. *A.I.R. Photo, Courtesy Davey Jordan Collection*

" The third 'promo' car remained street legal: it was never stripped and prepped for racing, nor cannibalized for its parts. **"**

This post-1968 Daytona race photo at the Daytona Beach Holiday Inn tells many stories. You can see all three A.I.R. L-88 Corvettes; two loaded onto their transport and ready for a trip back to Los Angeles. The third "PR" car is parked on the tarmac next to the No. 45 race car. Porsche No. 72 in the upper middle didn't fare so well; it was the victim of considerable front and rear driver-side body and suspension damage.

Notice the lack of giant, custom-built 18-wheel team transporters, which weren't yet the norm in the late 1960s. The transporter in the foreground, carrying the No. 44 car, comes from Gledhill Chevrolet, one of the team's sponsors. The dealership was located in Wilmington, California, just a few miles from the A.I.R. shop, and often served for team car deliveries and as a parts delivery conduit. *Photo Courtesy Davey Jordan Collection*

Judging from the non-running race car (left), with its rear wheels off and the tail jacked up in the air, you can tell that the 1968 Daytona was a very long 24 hours for the A.I.R. team. The pit was littered with nuts, bolts, torn-open oilcans, a helmet, and the other usual detritus of an endurance race that didn't go well. *Photo Courtesy Davey Jordan Collection*

The third "promo" car remained street legal: It was never stripped and prepped for racing, nor cannibalized for its parts. It was later sold into private hands, and after a succession of private owners, has been fully restored to pristine original condition. As of this writing it is proudly owned by Corvette enthusiast Steven Radke.

Formula A in 1969

At A.I.R.'s kick-off/cocktail/press conference party (held in Los Angeles on Monday, January 13, 1969), James Garner unveiled a rendering of the Formula A car being planned, designed, and built in cooperation with John Surtees. Surtees, a retired motorcycle racing champion and the 1965 Formula One champion with Ferrari, had become a race car constructor at the end of his open-wheel racing career. The car was introduced as the Garner TS-5. The Garner reference was obvious, the "T" stood for the car's accomplished racing car designer, Len Terry, the "S" stood for Surtees, and the "5" indicated the fifth generation of the design.

As mentioned earlier, the Formula A series was just a stutter step down from Formula One in terms of speed and technology; the cars were very fast and required considerable

You are cordially invited to the official opening of the new offices for James Garner's American International Racing Team on Monday, January 13th, 1969 3:30 to 5:30 p.m. 9255 Sunset Boulevard Suite 103 Los Angeles, California 90069 Tel: (213) 271-6149

A.I.R threw a fairly splashy cocktail party in Hollywood for its media/friends/sponsor launch event (you see footage of it in *The Racing Scene* documentary). James Garner greeted the crowd and unveiled a rendering for the team's under-development Formula A machine, the "Garner TS-5." *Photo Courtesy Davey Jordan Collection*

The Garner A.I.R. "PR/Backup L-88"

The L-88's potent 427 was a factory-offered racing engine, and not at all engineered for the unleaded, low-octane street gas that came along just a few years later. There was no unleaded gas at this time. *Photo Courtesy Richard Prince*

WARNING: VEHICLE MUST OPERATE ON A FUEL HAVING A MINIMUM OF 103 RESEARCH OCTANE AND 95 MOTOR OCTANE OR ENGINE DAMAGE MAY RESULT

The "PR car" was born much like the other A.I.R. team cars, but never got the racing headlight treatment or side pipes that the actual track cars wore. It would be difficult to imagine a more-handsome color for a Mako-bodied Corvette than this Le Mans Blue. *Photo Courtesy Richard Prince*

The L-88's massive Holley carb wanted cold air and lots of it, so a "cold air" hood was standard on the L-88 model. The air-cleaner housing nestles deeply into the scooped fiberglass hood. *Photo Courtesy Richard Prince*

The A.I.R. logo colors are red, white, and blue, and really pop off the Le Mans Blue paint. James Garner is a proud American and decorated war vet, so there was little question what his team colors would be. The "I" in "A.I.R." is particularly prominent in this logo, as if to differentiate James Garner's racing team from Dan Gurney's All American Racers (A.A.R.). The two are somewhat easily confused at times. *Photo Courtesy Richard Prince*

All three A.I.R. Corvettes were equipped with the heavy-duty power brakes option. This great detail shot shows the factory-level authenticity of the L-88's restoration: ultra clean, but not too shiny, using factory OEM parts and finishes. "Over restoration" is a common problem, as too many restoration shops confuse top-quality work with "better than new" condition or finishes, but this one looks just right. *Photo Courtesy Richard Prince*

The Garner A.I.R. "PR/Backup L-88"

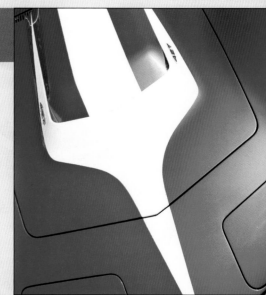

The restoration work on Steve Radke's A.I.R. Corvette is spectacular, using nothing other than original-equipment–spec parts, clamps, and hoses for maximum authenticity. A show winner now, if not a race winner in 1968. *Photo Courtesy Richard Prince*

I've not been able to verify the original inspiration for the "tines" or "tongs" graphic that makes up the A.I.R. logo, but to my eyes it's a dead ringer for the L-88's iconic "hood stinger" paint stripe treatment. *Photo Courtesy Richard Prince*

The wheels are the iconic magnesium American Racing TorqThrust, wearing equally iconic Goodyear BlueStreak racing tires. The cars came stock running silver-painted steel wheels with center caps and trim rings, but the racing L-88s ran this lighter, stronger mag, and it's a perfect period-correct look for this great car. *Photo Courtesy Richard Prince*

Here is a justifiably proud Steven Radke with his crown jewel among Corvettes, the A.I.R. "promo" L-88 roadster, restored to 1968 team-liveried glory. *Photo Courtesy Richard Prince*

Because the promo car was to remain street legal and licensed, it was saved from having its interior stripped to metal and a roll-cage installed, which would have been the first order of business had the car been chosen for race duty. Notice the blank plate where the audio system would be installed on a non-racing model; aficionados call this "radio delete" and the L-88 was also "heater delete" for the same reasons. All L-88 Corvettes of the day ran Muncie 4-speed manual transmissions. *Photo Courtesy Richard Prince*

Davey Jordan tests the Garner/Surtees TS-5 FA car at Riverside Raceway in April 1969. You can tell that this was at a fairly early stage in the car's development, because it wears no wings or airfoils, and uses Weber carburetors instead of fuel injection on its 5.0-liter Traco Chevy V-8. *Photo Courtesy Davey Jordan Collection*

skill to drive. Many of Europe's best sports car racers, several with Formula One experience on their resume, raced A, as did many Americans with Formula One aspirations. The Formula A series ran stand-alone races at many of America's best-known road courses, or occasionally shared a weekend race card with a sports car race, and ultimately morphed into what is more popularly known as Formula 5000.

Race car designers and builders of the day were just beginning to discover the use of aerodynamics, so some cars ran wings and spoilers while others did not. Here's James Garner's take on Formula A: "In Formula A, which is just a cut below Formula One, the cars can reach speeds of 180 mph. The A cars aren't easy to handle. They're too light overall, and the weight is in the back, so the rear end swings all over the place."

As noted, Garner planned to run his team from the pit, not the cockpit: "I couldn't drive in Formula A because I was busy working. Even if I'd had the time, the insurance companies wouldn't have covered me. For some reason, they did allow me to drive in the Baja 1000. I'm not sure why they made that exception. Maybe they thought it was a rally because there were checkpoints. Whatever the reason, I'm glad I fell through that crack."

He did visit England, where the Garner TS-5 was being developed and built, and he test-drove it on occasion, but he never raced it in competition. A.I.R. drivers Scooter Patrick and Davey Jordan were retained for driving duties, with Patrick running all of the races.

When Scooter speaks (middle), everybody listens, including team principal James Garner (left). Mechanic Bobby Fischetti (right) seems more intent on ministering to the car. Note the oil cooler mounted at the rear of the car, above the exhausts and the tops of the carbs, trying to maximize available windstream. *Photo Courtesy Davey Jordan Collection*

Perhaps not a good day at the races. Judging from Patrick's wrinkled brow and furtive stare (seated), and James Garner's scowl, things must not have been going well. The Formula A car has now sprung a high rear wing for additional cornering downforce, but still appears to run Weber carbs. *Photo Courtesy Davey Jordan Collection*

Garner (standing near driver-side rear wheel), Fischetti (standing in front of Garner), and Patrick (in car) on the pre-grid at St. Jovite, just before the pace lap. It was a full field of 26 cars that day, with David Hobbs starting on the pole and winning the race in a car very similar to the Garner team's TS-5. An accident put Patrick out of the race; although he wasn't seriously injured, the car suffered significant damage and ended A.I.R.'s 1969 season in Formula *Photo Courtesy Davey Jordan Collection*

This photo was most certainly taken at a test day, as the car wears no number. James Garner (middle) confers with Scooter Patrick (right) while mechanic Fischetti (to Garner's right) pays attention to the car. *Photo Courtesy Davey Jordan Collection*

Even though Davey Jordan and Scooter Patrick tested the TS-5 FA machine, only Patrick raced it during the A.I.R era. Here "Scoot" tests the car at Riverside International Raceway in April 1969 coming out of the famous Turn 6. *Photo Courtesy Davey Jordan Collection*

Prior to the Formula A race at Riverside in 1970, the series sponsored a press conference at a South Bay, California, restaurant owned by Dick Smothers. With him here is the fabulous race queen Candy Martin. *Photo Courtesy Davey Jordan Collection*

A.I.R.'s experience as a Formula A car builder and entrant was a mix of highs and lows, unfortunately with more of the latter than the former. They experienced teething problems at nearly every event; there were blown engines, other mechanical failures, wrecks, and all manner of roadblocks to A.I.R. achieving success. Moreover, the A series was difficult from a logistical standpoint, with tracks all over the United States plus a couple race dates in Canada, requiring lots of hauling, towing, and travel for the West Coast team.

Davey Jordan wished to continue with the program, post-A.I.R., as an independent owner/driver team, and neatly summarizes his own and A.I.R.'s Formula A experience: "At the end of the 1969 season, Garner took one of the Surtees cars and entered it in the races at Lime Rock Park and St. Jovite, with Scooter driving. The accident at St. Jovite ended their season." [Patrick was shaken up but not seriously injured, and the car was damaged but not irreparable.] Scooter never finished a race in the Garner/Surtees car.

John Crean [Fleetwood Motorhomes Company millionaire founder] bought three Eagles after the Surtees cars failed his test at Riverside Raceway in early 1969. Crean remembers, "We got the first Eagle in late 1969 and proceeded with a testing program. After the testing program was finished, [Jordan's wife] Norma and I took over and raced the Eagle in the first five races of the 1970 season. My only podium with the Eagle was a second to John Cannon, at Riverside." Crean disbanded the team after the fifth race.

Road Racing Two Lolas in 1969

By many accounts a somewhat brighter spot in A.I.R.'s brief history was its experience running road-racing prototype-class Lola T70s at Sebring and Daytona in 1969. As mentioned, A.I.R. sold its Corvettes after the one less-than-spectacular outing at the 24 Hours of Daytona in 1968, and purchased a pair of year-old Lola T70 Mk 3 sports racers. Many of the team engineers, mechanics, and drivers were retained for the 1969 season, with plans to run only in the two main long-distance endurance races. A.I.R. didn't have the funding or infrastructure to follow the series as it crisscrossed the United States.

The two white cars were refinished in A.I.R.'s signature dark blue with white stripe livery. German Can-Am and Formula A/5000 ace Lothar Motschenbacher was retained as an additional team driver, replacing both Caplan and Guldstrand. Traco once again built the 5-liter Chevrolet engines. The competition in the "big-bore" or 5-liter sports prototype category was fierce.

The Ford GT40, hot off of back-to-back-to-back wins at the 24 hours of Le Mans, was fast and reliable. Roger Penske fielded a new updated Lola, similar to A.I.R.'s machines but a year newer, driven by Mark Donohue; the Sports Car Club of America (SCCA), United States Road Racing Championship (USRRC), and Can-Am stalwart Chuck Parsons was a teammate.

For Daytona 1969, Ed Leslie and Lothar Motschenbacher were teamed in the No. 8 A.I.R. Lola, with Davey Jordan and Scooter Patrick paired in the No. 9 team car. Qualifying

> "The competition in the 'big-bore' or 5-liter sports prototype category was fierce.

David Hobbs. *Photo Courtesy Bill Warner*

David Hobbs was born June 9, 1939, in Royal Leamington Spa, England, and began racing professionally in the mid-1960s. He's an accomplished all-rounder, having competed and won in a wide variety of open-wheel formula classes and in sports cars, touring cars, Indy cars, IMSA, Can-Am, and Formula One. He has competed in the Indianapolis 500 and the 24 Hours of Daytona. He made twenty starts in the 24 Hours of Le Mans race, finishing in eighth place at the first attempt in 1962, following with a pole position and a best finish of third (in 1969 and 1984) to his credit. He drove in six Formula One Grands Prix for the BRM, Honda, and McLaren teams.

In 1971 Hobbs won the U.S. Formula 5000 L&M Continental Series championship driving for Carl Hogan in a McLaren M10B-Chevrolet. He won five of the eight rounds that year at Laguna Seca, Seattle, Road America (Elkhart Lake), Edmonton, and Lime Rock. A dozen years later, he claimed the 1983 Trans-Am Series championship as well. Hobbs made a pair of NASCAR Cup starts in 1976, and briefly led the Daytona 500 that year.

Hobbs has since retired from professional racing, but his observation is well known after serving as an expert commentator for SPEED television and NBC Sports covering Formula One. Younger enthusiasts may recognize him as the voice of the "David Hobbscap" character in the Pixar film, CARS 2.

James Garner, in the documentary The Racing Scene, *references that Hobbs nearly joined the A.I.R. team as a driver, but that for a variety of reasons, it didn't work out. Garner called him a great competitor and a damn good friend, often referring to him as "Davey" Hobbs. Why did Hobbs and A.I.R. never get together?*

In 1966, I started to drive for John Surtees in his Lola T70; this was the result of having driven one of the first T70s in 1965 for a private entrant. I had also been at a lot of the original testing of the 70 in late 1964, all of which was done by Surtees for Eric Broadley. I got to know Eric in 1963 when I drove the F Junior MK5 for quasi works team MRP, and I had a very good year, my first in open-wheel racing. This led to me driving the original Lola GT at Le Mans in 1965 with Richard Attwood, the star MRP driver, and also the richest! So, that is how I got to be involved with Lola and Surtees.

The 1966 and 1967 seasons with Surtees were pretty miserable; missed lots of races, short of funds, and all sort of political machinations, at which John was World Class.

So, fast forward to 1968 when I got a chance to drive the works Honda, the Hondola in the Italian GP, after practicing in the original air-cooled 3-liter car of their own design. For the race I was given the choice and chose the V-12 Lola chassis.

For 1969 John had become his own manufacturer and wanted me to drive his new Len Terry–designed F5000; so far so good. Even better, he was to do a deal with James Garner who was to run a two-car team in the Formula A U.S. championship run by the SCCA. Well, very early on this came unglued, broken promises abounded, I'm sure, although I have no real proof of anything. So as usual John's program was running very late.

I did a few races in the spring in the U.K. and in late June went to Ireland and won the race at Mondello Park from Mike Hailwood in a Lola.

Soon after that, John dispatched a car, a mechanic, and me to Bowmanville, Ontario, Canada, from where we mounted a campaign for the championship. We missed the first seven races but still came in second in the championship by one point, scoring more wins than anyone else. During the Formula A campaign I ran into James a few times as he did field a car. I don't remember him talking too much about the reason why the deal imploded. It might have been a sponsor he thought he had, a major motor home manufacturer from near Riverside, I think.

He was always very friendly to me and my family and it would have been so much better if he and John had done a deal. Why it never happened I don't know, but after four years with Surtees at that time, the finger of suspicion has to point to John, I'm afraid.

I don't know why James didn't race his own Lola sports cars. Maybe he just felt he wouldn't be quick enough. I can't really comment on his skills but he certainly was keen and, like Paul Newman, probably would have made a very good driver. Probably not as good as Paul, who was pretty extraordinary, considering he didn't start until in his forties.

Starting late, again, in 1970 the Surtees team came third. At the end of the season, having given Mark Donohue a good run a few times, Roger Penske asked me to share the Ferrari 512 with Mark in 1971 and to drive in the Indy 500, plus Pocono and Ontario, but I would have to change from Firestone to Goodyear and he would help find another F5000 owner.

Surtees went ballistic; I mean ballistic! None of his Formula One promises, or endurance, or even a proper crack at F5000 had materialized but he still thought I owed him my entire career. Anyway I won the F5000 championship easily in 1970 with Carl Hogan so I guess I made the right choice.

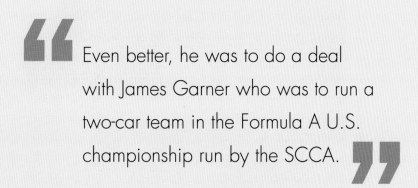

" Even better, he was to do a deal with James Garner who was to run a two-car team in the Formula A U.S. championship run by the SCCA. "

The Lola T-70 is as beautiful and nicely proportioned a sports racer as was ever built. There are very slight similarities between it and the Ford GT40, as Lola's Eric Broadley had a big hand in the Ford's early development. Notice the "peace sign" decals on the fender-mounted rearview mirrors. Hey, it was 1969 after all, not so long after the infamous "Summer of Love." *Photo Courtesy Bill Warner*

This wonderful grouping illustrates the variety and speed differentials of the car classes running at Daytona. The No. 8 A.I.R. Lola stalks a Mercury Cougar, an Alfa Romeo T 33-2, and a Porsche 911. *Photo Courtesy Bill Warner*

was dominated by the deeply talented and well-financed factory teams, with the A.I.R Lolas qualifying 11th and 10th respectively.

Endurance racing is much like Italian opera: long and full of drama. There's so much going on, and so many hours and laps during which anything can happen. A modern Formula One race is about 2 hours, start to finish. An average running of the Indy 500 today takes 2½ to 3 hours. Daytona and Le Mans run 24 hours, twice around the clock; Sebring lasts "just" a dozen. The chances for an accident or mechanical failure are huge in endurance racing, and every range of human condition is a factor: fatigue, mistakes at the wheel or in the pits, fuel or tire miscalculations, weather, physical trauma, you name it.

James Garner had the right perspective: "Just hold on to it; don't try to win it in the first hour, and don't break." He instilled this mantra into the minds and actions of his team. In his typical self-deprecating fashion, he also mused, "Here's your average movie actor taking on the factory teams; now think about that!"

"Nighttime is the right time" for endurance racing. The helmeted Jordan (left) has either just gotten out of the car or is preparing to get in it for his next stint at the wheel. James Garner, as always, is thoughtful. *Photo Courtesy Davey Jordan Collection*

> " Not a win in the purest sense, but since finishing any 24-hour enduro is a win of sorts; it was a commendable and encouraging result for the 'average movie actor's' efforts. "

The A.I.R. Lolas experienced their share of mechanical maladies, suspension problems, and overheating, but the crew kept their heads in the game and kept the machines alive; as did Garner's foursome of outstanding drivers. As the Porsches and Fords dropped out, the A.I.R. machines crept up the leader board. It paid off in a big way for the small team.

Donohue and Parsons, in Penske's well-funded and year-newer Lola, won the race, but the Leslie/Motschenbacher A.I.R. Lola No. 8 finished an impressive second overall, 30 laps down to the winners. Patrick and Jordan didn't fair quite as well, but kept themselves and their ailing car together for a credible seventh-place finish. Not a win in the purest sense, but since finishing any 24-hour enduro is a win of sorts, it was a commendable and encouraging result for the "average movie actor's" efforts. The team prepared and planned for the Sebring 12-hour race a month later, believing that an overall win was within their grasp.

It's difficult to compare the Sebring and Daytona races. Of course Sebring runs only half the number of hours, but it's a very different circuit; many will tell you it's tougher

Considering how poorly things went for the A.I.R. team at Daytona in 1968, its first time out with the Lolas in 1969 was credible. Not without problems, both cars were fast and ran well. This is the Jordan/Patrick No. 9 car, finishing seventh overall. *Photo Courtesy Bill Warner*

on cars and on drivers. Sebring, being a retired military airfield, was (back in the day) very rough and choppy; its mottled, bumpy surface was hell on suspensions and tires. So even though it was only half the number of hours as Daytona, the A.I.R. crew had its work cut out for it.

The car and driver lineups remained the same, as did much of the competition, with the exception of a lone factory-backed Ferrari 312, which did not run at Daytona. In spite of Motschenbacher's car blowing an engine in practice, the team packed up the night before the race tired but feeling good about its prospects.

Leslie and Motschenbacher in the No. 11 car at Sebring in 1969, which turned out to be A.I.R.'s final effort in the major endurance racing competition. They appeared to have a podium finish in hand, when last-minute mechanical woes dropped them to a hard-fought but ultimately disappointing sixth-place finish. *Photo Courtesy Bill Warner*

The Motschenbacher-Leslie Lola chases the Herrmann-Stommelen 908 at Sebring. The A.I.R. Lola finished a credible, although ultimately disappointing, sixth overall, while the Porsche roadster in its racing debut finished in third. *Photo Courtesy Bill Warner*

The Sebring race, held March 22, 1969, began well enough for the gleaming blue Lolas. Patrick and Jordan had more experience at Sebring than did their teammates, which should have bidden well for them, but their No. 10 machine didn't allow it. It overheated just a few hours into the race, and did not finish.

Motschenbacher and Leslie stormed on, slightly below everyone else's radar, as the Alfas, Porsches, and other cars experienced problems and fell aside. For a short while, Ed and Lothar were lapping as high as third, the car's No. 11 lighting up on the leader board. However, Sebring's punishing surface ultimately failed the left-side front hub and wheel bearing assembly, and required a long pit stop to repair.

As a harbinger of things to come at Le Mans later that year, Jacky Ickx and Jackie Oliver convincingly won Sebring in their JW Automotive Ford GT40, fast but never leading early in the race. Mario Andretti and Chris Amon finished second in their factory-backed Ferrari 312 P. Unfortunately, the lengthy pit stop for suspension repairs slid the remaining A.I.R. Lola off the podium for a still-credible but disappointing sixth-place overall finish.

Having only planned to run these two endurance races, Sebring 1969 was the final moment in A.I.R.'s all too brief run as a professional sports car road racing team, and James Garner called it a day as a racing team owner. In his autobiography, he said, "It was fun and exciting owning A.I.R. while it lasted, but I disbanded the team at the end of 1969 after discovering that racing is a big commitment of time and money. I didn't have enough of either to continue."

The Racing Scene

No discussion of A.I.R.'s racing endeavors would be complete without mention of *The Racing Scene*, a documentary following the trials, tribulations, and triumphs, as well as the humanity of A.I.R.'s 1969 racing seasons in Formula A and with the Lolas; the title sequence also features Garner and Patrick running the Baja 1000 as members of the Stroppe Ford Bronco team.

Garner's own Cherokee Productions, in cooperation with Filmways, produced this entertaining 90-minute documentary/feature film in 1970 "starring James Garner" and mostly narrated by him as well. Viewed in today's parlance, it's full of folksy, 1970s sayings such as "just mixing it up," "finding the groove," and "having what you think is a good idea, and making it work."

It's a beautifully made film, and any fan of sports car racing in the late 1960s and early 1970s will go a bit nuts over the fabulous race cars, street cars, and great period footage. However, what *The Racing Scene* does more than anything is underscore James Garner's passion for motorsport, and his humanity and compassion for his drivers and crew. In the narration he comments about how every time his drivers are on the track it "scares the hell out of him."

Motschenbacher and Leslie stormed on, slightly below everyone else's radar, as the Alfas, Porsches, and other cars experienced problems and fell aside.

This montage-style artwork was very typical of movie posters and magazine covers of the late 1960s. The buxom blonde in her "flower power" dress was also a thematic look of the era. *Photo Courtesy Matt Stone Collection*

This casual snapshot shows Scooter Patrick settling into the Garner TS-5 for a run at the L & M Continental Championship for Formula A cars at historic Lime Rock Park in Connecticut. The car is being wired with cameras and sound recording equipment for filming of *The Racing Scene*. The car experienced mechanical problems before the start of the race and could not qualify, so Patrick had to start from the pit lane, which put him nearly a half-mile behind the rest of the pack at the start. Patrick ultimately caught up with some of the backmarkers, before being taken out in a wreck. *Photo Courtesy Davey Jordan Collection*

Team owner James Garner, handsome and pensive as ever, felt he could do the most good for his A.I.R. team by helping from the pits, which he said publicly several times, instead of getting behind the wheel. *Photo Courtesy Bill Warner*

Of particular interest is how he appraises his drivers. About Lothar Motschenbacher, he says he's "Teutonic, quick tempered, and the all-out racer." He calls the late Ed Leslie "an old pro, at his peak, who's experienced everything. He knows everyone on the grid and what they're up to." Garner praises Scooter Patrick's abilities often, and it's clear that the team owner listens to Patrick's advice about how to set up the car and run the team. He calls Davey Jordan "Mr. Cool. He's methodical, one of the coolest guys I've ever met in my life," and when Davey gets ready to hit the track, "he shows no more emotion than a guy sitting down to a plate of eggs in the morning."

In the film Garner comments about it "taking $35,000 just to put a year-old Lola on the track," which of course was a lot of money in 1969 for any sort of car, racing or otherwise. He harrumphs a bit about replacement racing engines costing "five grand a piece," which, of course, in modern times likely wouldn't pay for a new engine in your street car, much less a Traco-built racing Chevy V-8.

The Racing Scene has not officially been released or distributed by the production company. If you are a sports car racing, and/or James Garner fan, it's a must see, if you can find it.

Both long retired, Davey Jordan and Scooter Patrick remain friends, and in touch with James Garner. Both drivers compliment Garner on his conduct and professionalism as a team owner, Jordan commenting that he never "tried to over-manage the team. Everyone was clear on what their jobs were, and Mr. Garner let them do it, helping where he could but never stepping on anyone's responsibilities. Within his means, James Garner gave his teams everything they needed to be competitive."

James Garner, Scooter Patrick, Lothar Motschenbacher, Dave Jordan, and Ed Leslie.

Also with drivers Parnelli Jones, John Surtees, Chris Amon, David Hobbs, Andrea deAdamich, Roger Penske, Mario Andretti, Sam Posey, Mark Donohue, John Cannon, George Wintersteen, and Bob Bondurant, with special appearances by Dick Smothers and Miss Continental Racing Queen Majken Kruse.

Directed by Andy Sidaris
Written by William Edgar
Produced by Barry Scholer
Music by Don Randi
Cinematography by Earl Rath
Sound by Pierre Adidge
Edited by James Gross
Associate Producer: Irvine Leonard
Technical Advisor: Donald Rabbitt
Production Coordination: Beverly Mulconery
In cooperation with Sports Car Club of America
A Cherokee Productions Barry Scholer-Andy Sidaris Presentation. A Filmways Picture

Actor/comedian Dick Smothers was another entertainer attracted to racing, seen here in the pits chatting with James Garner. The car is a Smothers' Porsche Carrera 6. Smothers is featured prominently in *The Racing Scene*, including his excellent narration of some in-car camera footage. Smothers raced Formula A, Can-Am, and the big endurance races. He wasn't terribly fast but was competent, safe, and didn't embarrass himself as a celebrity driver up against the pros. *Photo Courtesy Bill Warner*

Over time, at Sebring and Daytona, it wasn't so unusual for a team owner or other "gentleman racer" to take a stint at the wheel against the pros. I asked Patrick and Jordan if they knew why James Garner, an obviously talented and capable racing driver, didn't take a stint or two in one of his team's Lolas (he was already quite clear about why he didn't drive the Formula A machine).

Patrick's view is modestly contrary to other opinions that have been expressed about Garner's potential as a professional racing driver: "Don't get me wrong; Jim was a fabulous driver," Patrick says. "But remember, at the pro level, we were driving all out, 10 tenths, all the time, day in and day out, just to be competitive, which Jim did not; and don't forget that most of us were younger than he was too."

Jordan believes that Garner, with practice, would have been respectable at the wheel of the big British sports car. "But he probably didn't think that was his place, as the team owner. Like I said, he was good at letting everyone, including us drivers, do their job."

THE ROCKFORD FILES *A TV Classic*

The seminal Jim Rockford look, circa season one, 1974. James Garner never was more handsome, with the trademark shades, long-sleeved dress shirt, soda cup from a fast-food joint, and a gold 1974 Firebird. *Photo Courtesy H.L./ mptvimages.com*

"

Rockford's Firebird was a character in the show.

— *James Garner*

"

Television in America in the 1970s was filled with crime drama series, everything from *Kojak* to *Hawaii Five-O*. Without question, one of the most popular, and long-lived, is *The Rockford Files*, starring James Garner. The show began its weekly run in September 1974 and continued through July 1980, airing during prime time on Friday nights. It was wildly popular during its first six seasons, went into syndication immediately after its final prime-time episode, and hasn't been off the air since.

Chapter Five

Mr. Garner's Cherokee Productions produced 122 episodes of *The Rockford Files* for NBC/Universal, and upon syndication, it was translated and subtitled into many foreign languages. While James Garner was already among the world's most popular actors, *Rockford* brought him into millions of homes on a weekly basis, and also increased his international fan base exponentially.

Garner played private detective James S. Rockford, with the show boasting an interesting and varied cast of regulars and big-name guests. So many factors make it great, from crisp, fun, and occasionally brilliant writing to the fact that about half of the show was shot on location, at iconic and interesting Los Angeles–area locales. Particularly interesting was its Malibu, California, home

base: the parking lot of the Sand Castle restaurant in an area called Paradise Cove, where Rockford docked his massive, yet charmingly run down, single-wide house trailer. The show was a commercial smash and was awarded numerous Emmys.

While *Rockford* was by no means a "car based" show, any detective drama worth gum on its shoe features great action, whether it's the occasional fight scene, a few shots fired, or cool cars, and a car chase now and again. It began with Rockford's Pontiac Firebird Esprit. James Garner has often commented about being asked why Rockford didn't drive a Trans Am, the flashier, more performance-oriented Firebird. Mr. Garner says, "Well, it's not that he [Rockford] wouldn't have liked one, it's

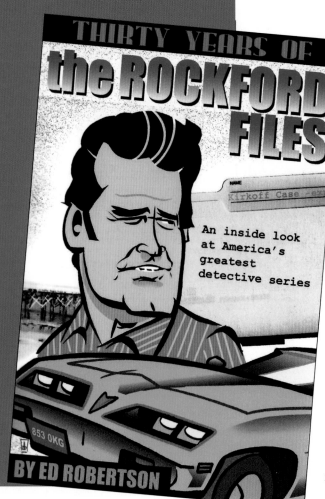

much sexier, but I didn't think he could afford it. The Firebird [Esprit model, used in the show] was more of a blue-collar car, a stripped-down version of the Trans Am. And I thought it handled better than the Trans Am."

The Firebird Deal

Pontiac supplied three Firebirds per season as is typical for television or movie production. One car is the "beauty" or "hero" car used for on-camera scenes when it needs to look pristine and for close-up shots with the actors; it is seldom put in risky shots or action situations. A second car is designated the "action" car for action shots, chase scenes, and such. The third is either usually a backup, or sometimes dubbed the "damage" car in case the script calls for the star's car to be wrecked or otherwise damaged.

One or another of the trio usually ends up being the "sound" car. It is equipped with a variety of microphones all around the exterior, and sometimes inside, to pick up road noise, the sounds of the car itself (a rumbling engine or squealing tires), and to aid in recording audio tracks of the actors when they are inside the cars.

Garner notes that the Firebirds were used much as equipped from the factory, with the exception of a little suspension stiffening to improve the handling for chase scenes. The cars, painted Sierra Gold, ran 400-ci V-8 engines and 3-speed automatic transmissions, but were otherwise standard production Firebird Esprits with a minimum of accessories and Camel Tan interiors.

For all but two episodes, Rockford's Firebird carried California blue-and-yellow license plate number 853 OKG, which was never officially released or issued by the California Department of Motor Vehicles. The number was reserved for *Rockford* filming use only.

Even though *The Rockford Files* wasn't purely about cars, its frequent car chases and car action were a big part of the show's charm, and certainly where actor/producer/racer/race team owner James Garner got to have some fun. Given his experience and talent at the wheel of an automobile, it was only natural that he got to do most of the driving as Rockford. This certainly made life easier for the directors and editors, not having to deal with the intricacies of another driver "doubling" Garner at the wheel. When the scene warranted it, stunt man, longtime friend, and occasional second-unit director Roydon Clark doubled James Garner as Rockford.

The Firebird was more than capable of keeping up during chase scenes and squealing its own tires when necessary. Garner tells the story of one of the show's trademark car

If you want to know the names of every writer, producer, creative team member, cast member, guest, and plotline of every episode of The Rockford Files, the best place to find it all is in Ed Robertson's Thirty Years of The Rockford Files. Several editions of this book are in release; all are good. However, the later editions, this one from a 2005 re-release, are the most comprehensive. Photo Courtesy Matt Stone Collection

moves, ultimately nicknamed the "Rockford," although he didn't invent it; it had been and continues to be used in a variety of television and movie scenes.

"It was really just a reverse 180, also known as a 'moonshiner's turn' or 'J-turn.' When you're going straight in reverse at about 35 mph, you come off the gas pedal, go hard left, and pull on the emergency brake. That locks the rear wheels and throws the front end around. Then you release everything, hit the gas, and off you go in the opposite direction."

One wonders if a young James Garner might have worked on that move when playing "ditch 'em" with his friends on the back roads surrounding Norman, Oklahoma.

How did the whole Firebird deal come about? Eric Dahlquist, Sr., product placement and media relations executive with Vista Group, was involved in many promotional and public relations initiatives for General Motors during the 1970s. He recalls, "Pontiac

Looking pristine again is one of the 1977 Firebirds used in the taping of *The Rockford Files*. It was acquired in somewhat sad shape, but beautifully and authentically restored by Rockbird enthusiast Pat McKinney. *Photo Courtesy Mel Stone*

This is the license plate *Rockford* fans know by heart. It is actually a "stunt plate," which is real in terms of look, size, and materials to those issued by the Department of Motor Vehicles, even though this sequence of numbers and letters wasn't issued as a real consumer license plate at the time. *Photo Courtesy Mel Stone*

Marketing did a lot of its own product placement deals back then and therefore I was not involved in putting the initial project together. Vista ultimately did a lot of work with James Garner's Cherokee Productions, by virtue of the latter's use of GMC trucks, also represented by Vista Group." In addition, Vista also lent support to Cherokee regarding the Firebirds in the event of service or repair needs.

Action Scenes

The car chases in *Rockford* are relatively tame compared to the all-time greats in *Bullitt, Ronin*, or the *Jason Bourne Trilogy*, but they were credible. The producers obviously put some effort into rooting them in certain automotive realities, thus maintaining some credibility and integrity with knowledgeable automotive fans in the audience. For example, in one episode, Rockford gets involved in a car chase with a "baddie" at the wheel of a Jaguar E-Type. As you'd expect, Rockford outdrives him by a fair margin, and ultimately the bad-guy driver loses control of the Jag, and flips it over onto its roof.

A later scene shows the overturned car to be a real E-Type; many other producers likely wouldn't have gone to the effort and expense of procuring a real E-Type and putting it upside down; they may have settled for the least expensive, similarly sized and colored car they could find quickly and easily. However, to its credit, the *Rockford* production team made the effort of flipping and showing the bottom side of a genuine Jaguar E-Type.

Watching the show today is great fun for classic and collector car enthusiasts, as the scenes are filled with so many great old cars. Most of the Los Angeles Police Department squad cars used in the show were AMC Matadors, American Motors' (now long out of business) large, somewhat frumpy sedan. It's funny, though, that the inspectors and detectives usually drove full-sized Fords, such as LTDs. And invariably, the wealthy West Los Angeles characters (writers, producers, attorneys, villains, and such) drove the very latest Mercedes-Benz sedans and sports cars, most of which today are sought-after collectibles.

You see lots of great car play in the series pilot, where Rockford's Firebird chases a couple of bad guys and their Plymouth sedan out of town and through the desert, until they dump the car and board a small aircraft. Also check out the Season Two episode called "Gearjammers," a two-parter. Season Three's "House on Willis Ave." is also a two-parter with some good driving action, and Season Five's "Never Send a Boy King to Do a Man's Job" puts Rockford at the wheel of a Can-Am–style racing car, obviously no stretch for Garner to play.

Some of the car play is downright funny. One particular chase scene comes to mind, when Rockford's Firebird is absent for repairs. He's at the wheel of a mid-1970s Chevrolet Caprice Classic coupe, a massive, heavy automobile not known for great roadholding or handling. The bad guy is driving the requisite same-era Cadillac, also no sports car. When pushed hard in a high-speed chase, the cars resemble whales attempting ballet; they lean over hard demonstrating excessive and almost unsafe body roll, their smallish whitewall tires howling

Two very interesting guys with a pair of very special cars. On the left is Eric Dahlquist, Sr., former editor of *Hot Rod* and *Motor Trend* magazines, and longtime public relations and product placement executive and principle of Vista Group. At right, of course, is James Garner. The car in the foreground is a General Motors Design Study based on the new-for-1979 Pontiac Firebird styling, loosely referred to as the Kammback Trans Am. The abruptly chopped-off Kamm tail pays homage to the work of pre–World War II–era German aerodynamicist Dr. Wunibald Kamm. The *Rockford*-spec Firebird in the background is likely a 1978; it was the car still in use in the production when the 1979 concept car was built. *Photo Courtesy Vista Group*

Rockbirds of a feather, flock together. These are three of the cars actually used in the filming of the show, from three different years/seasons. At left is a 1978 Firebird Esprit; in the middle, and nearly fully restored, is a 1977; and on the right, with the blue replacement hood, is a 1976 model Firebird Esprit, the only one among them running a genuine Pontiac-spec 400-ci V-8. *Photo Courtesy Mel Stone*

in protest. I can only imagine that our favorite protagonist was happy to get his Firebird back.

Another funny chase scene puts Rockford at the wheel of one of the most popular automotive punching bags of the 1970s, a Chevrolet Vega. This particular Vega was a bright blue rental, as Rockford was working a case in Arizona. Someone is out to hurt or kill Rockford, and gives chase in an unloaded, likely souped-up Diesel semi truck.

The hapless Vega was never a fast, powerful, or good handling car in base level form; this one is equipped with a standard 4-cylinder engine and automatic transmission. Rockford has his hands more than full keeping ahead of the long-haul tractor (hardly the fastest thing on ten wheels). Nevertheless, the ever-capable (and often lucky) James S. Rockford, Private Investigator, manages to get away unscathed.

In case you ever wonder how important a character the gold Firebird is among the Rockford cast, consider that the car appears no less than nine times in the opening title

sequence. It shows a variety of iconic scenes and locations around Los Angeles plus a variety of still shots of Garner as Rockford. It's possible the Firebird appears a tenth time; one snippet shows Rockford and another character plus the window line and trim of an automobile. However, the editing, timed to the theme music, is fast-paced at this point and it is difficult to verify if the car in the frame is the Firebird or not. The Firebird flashes through the sequence at least nine times, so the producers certainly weren't hiding it.

James Garner is, if nothing else, a loyalist. He often employed friends in key roles in his production company (and, key members of his production company often became his friends). Two examples are Roydon Clark, Garner's frequent stunt double and occasional action sequence driver-double, and Luis Delgado, reputed to be Garner's best friend, who played a Los Angeles Police officer on the show, and often joined him at various off-road races.

> "Nevertheless, the ever-capable (and often lucky) James S. Rockford, Private Investigator, manages to get away unscathed."

In spite of the production team's considerable efforts to keep the automotive action credible, there are some charming continuity goofs from time to time when it comes to cars. In one episode, Rockford is driving the criminal's Lincoln Continental sedan. The Lincoln first shown in-scene is a 1972–1973 model; the bad guy rides in the front passenger seat with Rockford driving at gunpoint. The two men argue and tussle, and the villain shoots Rockford in the arm. Then, in quintessential chase-scene fashion, the car careens off a modest cliff and down an embankment.

However, there is one problem and a somewhat amazing result: While the car that starts off the cliff was the 1972–1973 Continental, the one that actually flies over it and down the hill magically became a 1965 model. This is something the average viewer may or may not notice, but eagle-eyed car enthusiasts do, have, and will. It was likely a budgetary, timing, or car availability compromise: In 1974, a newer Lincoln was still somewhat expensive. Wrecked or otherwise not roadworthy, the 1965 models were commonplace and much more affordable; and therefore a less expensive alternative for tossing a car off a cliff.

One of the more amusing continuity flubs made on the show concerned a factual boo-boo in the show's opening "answering machine" sequence during one 1979 episode. Rockford fans are familiar with the brief, clever scene at the opening of the show where the camera pans over Rockford's desk. The phone rings and is picked up by Rockford's answering machine: "Hi. This is Jim Rockford. Leave your name and message and I'll get back to you." The caller is usually a potential client, or a creditor of one sort or another. In this particular instance, the caller is advising Rockford that a loan, partially collateralized by his car, is due, and that his car is going to be repossessed (or that he can "drop it off"). He referenced the car as "your 1979 Firebird." Except that Jim Rockford never drove a *1979* Firebird. All of the Firebirds used in the original filming of *The Rockford Files* TV series were 1974–1978 models.

For the 1979 model Firebird, Pontiac radically redesigned the front end styling of the car, and the new look was reputedly not to Garner's taste, so even during the filming of the 1979 season, 1978 model cars were used. Therefore, there's no way the mythical calling creditor could repossess Rockford's "1979 Firebird." It's a small detail, but a significant oops to those who follow such minutiae.

Another modest automotive detail flub is in one episode in which someone driving a 1973–1974 Chevrolet Nova is following Rockford; he calls the Department of Motor Vehicles, asking for information about someone in a "1967 Chevy." Of course, Chevrolet did produce a Nova in 1967, but it looks nothing like the 1974 model used. Jim Rockford apparently didn't know this, but it's likely that James Garner did, or perhaps should have? No matter, that episode had some particularly good car play in it. Guest actor Sharon Gless drove a sporty blue Morgan Plus 4. The Paradise Cove parking lot (where Rockford's housetrailer is parked) contained a Jaguar E-Type Series I 2+2. A pair of FBI agents

> "
>
> Hi. This is Jim Rockford. Leave your name and message and I'll get back to you.
>
> "

followed Rockford in a mid-1970s Chrysler coupe as big as any period Caddy or Lincoln. And the mob guys met up with Rockford aboard a Mercedes-Benz 600 Pullman limo.

GMC Trucks

No discussion of *The Rockford Files* on-set vehicles would be complete without mentioning GMC trucks. For most years the show was being filmed each week and GMC light- and medium-duty trucks toted the equipment and crew from locale to locale. In addition, Rockford's father, Rocky, portrayed by the late Noah Beery, Jr., drove a customized GMC pickup, and very often, so did James Garner.

The first was the blue and white early-1970s GMC half ton, described in Chapter One. It also appeared, briefly, in at least one *Rockford* episode. There is a mild implication that this blue and white GMC was Rocky's but it was soon supplanted by what Rockfordphiles consider the "real" Rocky truck: a medium silver gray with red/maroon trim 1976 GMC Sierra Classic, customized by Vic Hickey. Its build and spec is described in the January 1977 issue of *Truck & Van Ideas* magazine.

Editor Bob Beaver noted that the truck "runs a warmed-over 400-ci engine, Turbo 400 automatic [transmission], 3.73 rear end, and a four-wheel-drive setup from the factory. Hickey added the winch, brush guard, hub covers, side step plates in the bed, auxiliary gas tanks (52 gallons total), and custom steering wheel. Cibie driving lights are fitted on the front bumper and rear roll bar (another Hickey item). The cab boasts a Pace CB radio, and the exterior paint is silver with maroon panels and orange pinstriping." It is occasionally confused with the red pickup that GMC provided to Garner (discussed in Chapter One), but they are without question two different vehicles.

The "Rocky" truck wasn't just set decoration; it appeared in several *Rockford Files* chase scenes and action sequences. Once filming ceased in 1980, Robert Harris, a *Rockford* fan from Florida, just had to have it, and so his wife wrote a pair of letters to NBC asking to buy the truck. The direct and persistent approach was rewarded when he was ultimately allowed to purchase it; he and his wife went to California in Spring 1980, met with James Garner, completed the deal, and reportedly had a grand time of it.

The couple was photographed with James Garner and the truck. They were the lucky benefactors of Garner's considerable hospitality, and also received a pair of Los Angeles Lakers game

James Garner and the "Rocky" GMC on the cover of *Van Ideas* magazine, which included a brief feature and more photos describing the truck's build. As done with the *Rockford*-spec Firebirds, some enthusiasts build tribute/replica versions of this truck. *Photo Courtesy Pat McKinney Collection*

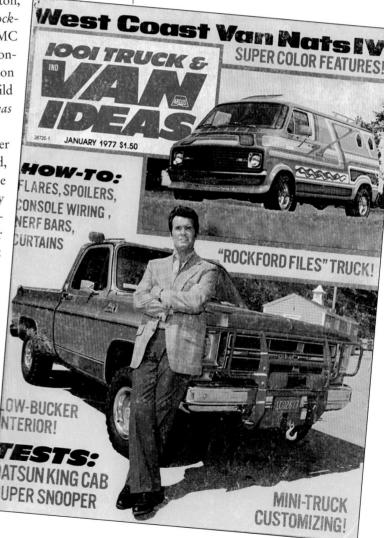

James Garner, again with the "Rocky" GMC at Paradise Cove in Malibu, California. So much of *The Rockford Files* was filmed there because Rockford parked his large, long, charmingly run-down single-wide house trailer there. *Photo Courtesy Vista Group*

James Garner with the Hickey-customized GMC he often drove as personal transport. Construction of the red and maroon GMC came along a few years later. *Photo Courtesy Vista Group*

Vista Group public relations and GMC produced this poster celebrating the brand's providing a variety of medium- and heavy-duty trucks to Cherokee Productions for use in the transportation and production of *The Rockford Files*. In the foreground is the customized GMC built for and provided to James Garner. Just behind it, to the right, is the gray and maroon customized GMC driven by Rockford's father (Rocky) on the show. *Photo Courtesy Vista Group*

tickets. Robert Harris and his wife flew to Los Angeles, and were met at the airport by Vista Group's Chuck Koch (see Chapter One). The couple also visited Malibu's Paradise Cove, where so much of *The Rockford Files* was filmed, and where the truck was often parked. The couple then drove the official Rocky GMC back home to Florida, and as of this writing, Robert Harris still owns it.

More *Rockford Files*, and More Rockford Firebirds

In spite of the fact that production of *The Rockford Files* television series ceased in 1980, people couldn't get enough of Jim Rockford, or James Garner playing him. By the early 1990s, television was on a bit of a nostalgia kick and every *Rockford* fan wanted a comeback. Because of previous legal skirmishes, it certainly wasn't going to happen with NBC, but ultimately, CBS convinced James Garner that the character was still viable, and persuaded him to reprise this most beloved television role in a series of "long form," two-hour "made-for-TV movies" as they were called at the time. Thus, Rockford returned in eight (although the original plan was for only a half dozen) TV specials that aired from 1994 to 1996, two decades after the birth of the original series.

In the early 1990s, Steve Reich was a young car enthusiast, working for Cinema Vehicle Services, an active provider of cars, trucks, and other motorized craft to the television

"
They were lucky the benefactors of Garner's considerable hospitality, and also received a pair of Los Angeles Lakers game tickets.
"

James Garner personally and officially turns the "Rocky" GMC truck over to its new owners, Floridians Mr. and Mrs. Robert Harris, who flew out just for the occasion, visited numerous *Rockford Files* locations, and then drove the truck home. Harris comments that he still has the truck, but not the same wife. *Photo Courtesy Vista Group*

- The show debuted on NBC on September 13, 1974, a Friday.
- The character of Rockford was originally written in an unproduced script for the ABC series *Toma*. That script was rewritten as the pilot for *The Rockford Files*. Both ABC (which initially rejected the script for *Toma)* and NBC had problems with the *Rockford* scripts. Executives at both networks thought the dramatic series scripts were too funny. The writers were always ordered to take out the funny lines. The writers and eventually the star refused. In addition, the character's original name was Tom, but James Garner insisted that he didn't sound like a "Tom" so it was changed to James.
- Many first-season stories were credited to "John Thomas James": a pen name for Roy Huggins. The name comes from the first names of Huggins' three sons.
- Three cast members from the series *Magnum, P.I.* (Tom Selleck, Roger E. Mosley, and Larry Manetti) did guest spots on *The Rockford Files*. An episode of *Magnum* features a discussion of a *Rockford Files* episode.
- David Chase, a writer/producer for *Rockford*, went on to create *The Sopranos*. An episode from *The Sopranos*' first season shows a scene in a retirement home in which the residents are watching television. We can't see what they're watching but we can hear the theme to *Rockford* playing clearly.
- The character of Rockford's father was named Joseph; he was named after writer Stephen J. Cannell's father. "Rockford" was used after Cannell found the name listed in the Universal Studios employee directory.
- The show was a co-production between the production companies of Roy Huggins, James Garner, and Universal. Garner sued Universal claiming he was not being paid his share of the syndication profits [together with issues of questionable accounting]. After several years of litigation, Universal settled with Garner.
- James Garner explained in an interview that Jim Rockford's license plate number, 853 OKG, was created by his agent at the start of the show and stands for August 1953, when Garner got his first acting job; OKG stands for Oklahoma Garner, his home state.
- The character of Richie Brockelman (played by Dennis Dugan) first appeared on this series. That appearance led to the short-lived series *Richie Brockelman, Private Eye*.
- Angel (played by Stuart Margolin) worked for the newspaper published by his brother-in-law Aaron Kiel. Aaron later became deputy police chief.
- In addition to detectives Richie Brockelman and Lance White, other recurring characters on the show were reformed prostitute Rita Kapkovic (played by Rita Moreno), disbarred lawyer John "Coop" Cooper (played by Bo Hopkins), Jim's ex-cellmate Gandolph "Gandy" Fitch (played by Isaac Hayes), and parole officer turned private investigator Marcus "Gabby" Hayes (played by Louis Gossett, Jr.).
- Jim was a Korean War veteran.
- Plans to spin the characters of Gandolph "Gandy" Fitch and Marcus "Gabby" Hayes off onto their own series were discussed, but they never came to fruition.
- Rockford's friends had a number of nicknames for him. His father called him "Sonny," the policeman Dennis Becker called him "Jimbo," and Gandolph Fitch's nickname for Jim was "Rockfish."
- Even though Rockford didn't have a permit to carry a gun, he did have one that he kept either in the cookie jar or in the coffee canister in his kitchen. "The coffee keeps it from rusting."
- Rob Reiner guest starred in an episode as a washed-up football quarterback. To separate himself from his *All in the Family* (1971) character, Reiner played this part without his hairpiece.
- The character Joseph "Rocky" Rockford was ranked No. 45 in *TV Guide's* list of the "50 Greatest TV Dads of All Time" (June 20, 2004, issue).

- Before becoming a regular as Lieutenant Doug Chapman in the fall of 1976, James Luisi made guest appearances during the first two seasons, usually as a criminal or another *Rockford* antagonist.
- Jim Rockford's favorite food was tacos. In fact, he could be seen having them for breakfast in many episodes.
- When the show was being developed, actor Robert Blake was considered for the lead. He was cast instead in *Baretta*, also created by Stephen J. Cannell.
- During the opening credits, when Rockford's answering machine message is heard just before the music starts, his telephone number is shown to be 555-2368. This was also the phone number shown for the *Ghostbusters* in their in-movie ad.
- The address of Jim Rockford's trailer was 29 Cove Road, Malibu. During the first season, Rockford's trailer moved from a parking lot just off Pacific Coast Highway in Malibu, California, to another Malibu location in an area known as Paradise Cove. The trailer remained at the Paradise Cove location for the remainder of the series. The address of the first location was 22968 Pacific Coast Highway, Malibu, California. The second address was approximately 28128 Pacific Coast Highway, Malibu, California.
- Rockford drove a Pontiac Firebird Esprit, not a Trans Am.
- Even though Tom Atkins' character is "Alex Diel" early in the series, later episodes show him working out of an office with "Lieutenant Thomas Diehl" stenciled on the door.
- In an early episode from the first season when Jim calls the police station and asks for Dennis he calls him "Lieutenant Becker." The character was actually Sergeant Becker for the next several seasons until Dennis was promoted to Lieutenant.
- Robert Donley, who played Joseph "Rocky" Rockford, played him only in the pilot episode. The role subsequently went to Noah Beery, Jr.

and movie industry. Reich remembers meeting with the show's transportation coordinator, Steve Hellerstein, who was responsible for all the vehicles seen on the show, as well as movements, schedules, and the transportation of the crew and cast. The goal was to find and acquire a trio of 1978 non–Trans Am–model Firebirds with automatic transmissions, power windows, and power locks. The colors were largely unimportant, as the team figured it would have to repaint the exteriors and retrim the cabins to get them right anyway (not at all uncommon in the movie and TV car business, as colors are changed all the time by the companies who provide picture car vehicles).

Reich recalls that there were some early discussions about using a then-current 1994–1996 model Firebird, which Pontiac likely would have provided and supported at no cost, but that idea quickly washed out. Reich notes that "Jim just liked the look of the 1977–1978 car, so we had to find that model," and that everyone agreed that the iconic gold 1970s body style was just "more Rockford." Three appropriate Firebirds were located in Southern California through newspapers and classified magazines such as the *Auto Trader*.

All three cars were in less-than-spectacular shape, but they were the right model and body style, each with a V-8 engine, air conditioning, and automatic transmission. Reich recalls that one of the cars was a special-order model called a "Red Bird" and was red from stem to stern, which required a comprehensive cosmetic restoration to get it looking good and in the right colors. He adds that General Motors' dealerships were helpful in sourcing parts to restore the cars (although the automotive aftermarket had not yet begun making much of a selection of reproduction parts for these cars in the mid-1990s).

No particular consideration was paid to engine performance or suspension tuning of these cars. "Since James Garner and Jim Rockford had both aged a bit since the mid-1970s, there was going to be less car chasing in the made-for-TV movies than in the original television series." Perhaps the classic Rockford J-Turn and squealing tires were deemed less appropriate for a "more mature" Jim Rockford in the 1990s than they were two decades previous. Who knows? Regardless, Cinema Vehicle Services provided, supported, and maintained the three new "Rockbirds" throughout CBS's filming of the eight *The Rockford Files* movies.

Actually, there was a fourth, or parts of a fourth, used for filming one of the movies. Reich recalls, in *Thirty Years of The Rockford Files*, "One Firebird you'll probably never see on display is the one featured in the first [CBS] reunion movie, *I Still Love L.A.* That vehicle, as you may recall, spent more time on the shelf than on the streets. We used a fourth car for that show only, it was a car we bought for parts, and had been stripped. When we saw what they had in mind for Rockford's car we took the shell of that extra car, painted it to look like the Firebird, and used it on the show." Reich also recalls that the exterior gold paint color on this newer batch of cars wasn't a perfect match of the 1974–1978 original, but certainly close enough for the movies.

Several of the cars and trucks used in the making of the television series have survived, today enjoyed by enthusiastic *Rockford* fans and car collectors, but Reich does not know what happened to the three Firebirds that he and Cinema Vehicle Services built. Reich has been consistent in making a life out of cars and Hollywood stars; he currently spends a great deal of time working with car collector extraordinaire Jay Leno in the management of his fabulous car and motorcycle collection.

Pat McKinney and the Bird's Nest

Southern California car guy Patrick McKinney claims no personal celebrity or connection to James Garner and the production and filming of *The Rockford Files* than being a huge fan of the star, the car, and the show. Like many guys of a certain age, he says, "I grew up watching *The Rockford Files,* and thought that gold Firebird was the coolest thing." So now he owns not one or two but *three* of the original Firebirds used by Cherokee Productions and Universal in the production of the original TV series. Now, that's a fan!

The point here is that even the average enthusiast, given loads of patience, tenacity, good manners, good research skills, a lot of luck, and good timing, can locate and acquire something special. The first of this trio acquired was his 1977 Rockbird. The second

> "Jim just liked the look of the 1977–1978 car, so we had to find that model."

Southern California *Rockford Files* enthusiast Patrick McKinney owns three cars that were actually used in the production of the show. From left are an unrestored 1978 model, the now completely restored 1977 Esprit, and wearing a blue replacement hood and also awaiting restoration is a 1976 Firebird. In case you are wondering, it is the 1977–1978 design that was made even more popular by the *Smokey and the Bandit* films. *Photo Courtesy Mel Stone*

was a similarly styled 1978, and finally the 1976 model. The 1976 is powered by a Pontiac 400-ci V-8; as was Pontiac's practice at the time, each of the other two is powered by a factory installed Oldsmobile 403 V-8. Remember, this was during the time when California had different emissions standards than the rest of the country. Pontiac began installing the Olds 403 in certain Firebird configurations; the proper Pontiac 400 put out more power but also had higher emissions ratings. It was still used in 4-speed Firebirds, but since the *Rockford* cars were all automatics, and California state cars, two got the Olds 403.

McKinney's 1977 is particularly interesting; it was used as the "sound car" during production. As he stripped away the paint, he was able to locate all of the mounting locations for the various microphones and sound equipment used to capture street sounds, the sounds of other cars, as well as the Firebird's own tire noise and rumbling V-8.

A proud McKinney stands in front of his 1977 Rockbird and models an original crewmember jacket obtained from sound engineer John Carter. *Photo Courtesy Mel Stone*

This massive, kind of ramshackle, single-wide isn't the actual double-door coach that Jim Rockford lived in, parked in a parking lot in Paradise Cove, California, but it's a close facsimile. It may not have been as famous a cast member as Rockford's Firebird, but it was nearly as popular.

Rockbird owner Pat McKinney located this scruffy trailer in a Southern California storage yard, and parked his 1978 Rockbird in front of it for this photo. The Firebird will be restored to pristine original condition; what fate awaits the trailer? *Photo Courtesy Jim Suva*

The basic model Firebird and the Esprit used for *The Rockford Files* wear much simpler jewelry and adornment than does the top-model Trans Am. Garner opined that Rockford likely would have liked to have the flashier, more expensive Trans Am, but he didn't feel that this particular private eye, who always seemed to be short of cash, could really afford it. *Photo Courtesy Mel Stone*

The small microphones plugged into this three-pronged outlet weren't particularly well hidden. If you watch the show carefully you'll spot them. McKinney confirmed that his car was in fact used for sound. When he was stripping the car down for paint, he found that the microphone pickup points had been removed; their holes had been covered over with body filler and paint during a previous paint job. *Photo Courtesy Mel Stone*

McKinney's 1977 has the unique distinction of being a "sound car" on the set of *The Rockford Files*. It was wired, inside and out, for a variety of lavaliere microphones in order to pick up the car's own sounds, plus that of other cars, street scenes, and so on. Here you can see the microphone's mounting plug at the lower leading edge of the passenger-side fender. *Photo Courtesy Mel Stone*

McKinney acquired the cars in common ways, such as perusing the pages of the *Auto Trader* classifieds, and one of the cars was bought on eBay. All were generally original when he purchased them but not in great shape. One had been locked away and all but lost in a storage facility in Riverside, California. One had been painted charcoal gray at some time or another was about to be stripped, cut up, and modified into some sort of racing car at the hands of its previous owner. Fortunately McKinney rescued them all before a single cutting torch was lit.

The three Rockbirds were acquired over several years and all needed restoration. The 1977 was first into the nest, so it was first into the fountain of youth. McKinney stripped the car to its nubbins, then refurbished and rebuilt it from the ground up one system at a time. During the time of our photo shoot, its primary restoration was substantially complete; the interior and engine compartment still needed final assembly, to appear in stock, original, "as new" condition.

Fortunately there's a fervent aftermarket reproduction parts business that services Camaros and Firebirds of this era. Although McKinney attempted to preserve and refurbish

as many factory original parts as possible, he replaced what could not be acceptably refinished or restored. If there's such a thing as a "concours restored" 1977 Pontiac Firebird Esprit, this is it.

This Rockbird was scheduled to be completed, running, and back on the road again as this book went to press. Online forums, chat rooms, eBay, and his circulation in the wide world of *Rockford* fans has enabled McKinney to assemble an impressive collection of *Rockford Files* clothing and ephemera. This will make for a more comprehensive display when he is ready to share his cars and truck at car shows.

McKinney is only in his fifties; not likely to be retiring any time soon, but when he does, restoring the 1976 and 1978 *Rockford* Firebirds will keep him well occupied. Not to mention the GMC 4x4 he owns, with plans to restore it to the spec and style of the silver gray and maroon "Rocky truck." No rocking chairs for this *Rockford* fan.

Understanding why *The Rockford Files* has enjoyed such loyal and long-legged worldwide popularity is easy. It was a particularly well-blended mix of the right idea and the right time, an engaging cast and great guest stars, catchy, clever writing, a superbly professional production team, supportive producers, cool locales, a hot gold Firebird, and a couple of handsome, affable guys named Jim.

The 1976 is a handsome design; some enthusiasts opine it was James Garner's personal favorite. McKinney's 1976 is a very complete car, but suffers severe rust damage and its restoration will be complex and expensive. But this *Rockford* enthusiast is undaunted; without question he plans to get around to restoring all three of his Rockbirds to pristine condition. *Photo Courtesy Mel Stone*

McKinney's 1978 isn't as rusty as the 1976, and shows evidence of a previous cheap gray paint job, but all will be put right and proper during its restoration. Recall that the 1978 model lived on during *Rockford's* two final seasons, as the production company never placed the 1979–1980 Firebirds into *Rockford* service during those years. This look was placed back into service for the production of made-for-TV movies in the 1990s. *Photo Courtesy Mel Stone*

The 1978's interior differs in subtle ways from that of some of the earlier cars. This car has a small Firebird emblem on the instrument panel just above the heater controls, and it has no tach, just a clock. This interior is very complete and original, but will still need a complete refurb upon restoration. *Photo Courtesy Mel Stone*

The blue paint and long oil-filler neck give this engine away as a 403-ci Olds V-8, used as a "400" in many mid- and late-1970s Firebirds as a way to skirt certain emissions issues. Regardless, it's a great engine, not quite as powerful in this tune as Pontiac's own 400, but zippy enough for Rockford. McKinney's reassembly of this car was nearly complete at the time of this photo shoot, and this golden bird promises to be back on the road soon. *Photo Courtesy Mel Stone*

Details are what make a car restoration great, or all wrong. Some of these underhood stickers are now made in reproduction, while others are still available as factory new-old-stock. Either way, they give a car the proper look and feel of a factory-original job. McKinney's car has all the right touches, looking much as General Motors built it in 1977. *Photo Courtesy Mel Stone*

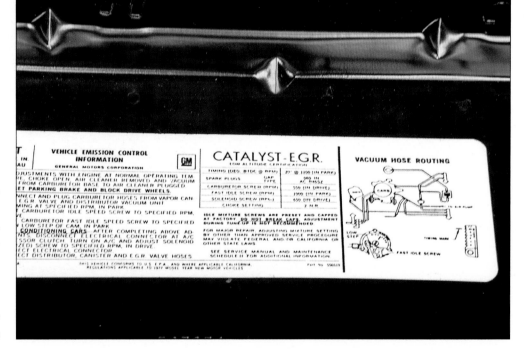

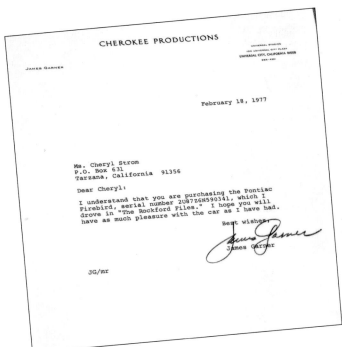

CHEROKEE PRODUCTIONS

JAMES GARNER

UNIVERSAL STUDIOS
100 UNIVERSAL CITY PLAZA
UNIVERSAL CITY, CALIFORNIA 91608

February 18, 1977

Ms. Cheryl Strom
P.O. Box 631
Tarzana, California 91356

Dear Cheryl:

I understand that you are purchasing the Pontiac Firebird, serial number 2U87Z6N590341, which I drove in "The Rockford Files." I hope you will have as much pleasure with the car as I have had.

Best wishes,

James Garner

JG/mr

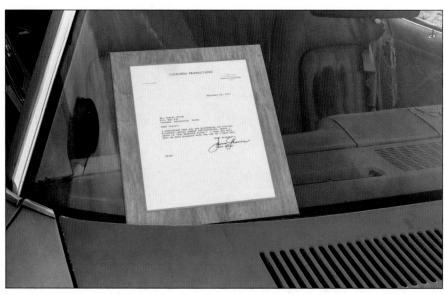

The woman who bought the 1976 Firebird, after its use on the show, asked the production company for a letter of authenticity signed by James Garner. Garner complied, providing proof of the car's use for the show and of his enjoyment of it. *Photo Courtesy Mel Stone*

Further evidence of the former life of McKinney's 1977 Esprit as an on-set "sound car" is several holes drilled in the floorpan to run wires to all the outboard microphone locations. The holes are relatively small, and he left them beneath the new carpeting as documentation of the car's provenance. *Photo Courtesy Mel Stone*

As part of the restoration, the cabin of McKinney's 1977 was stripped down nearly as far as it could be, then painted and recarpeted. The dash, console, and rest of the upholstery will complete the multi-year process. *Photo Courtesy Mel Stone*

All of the *Rockford* Firebirds ran Pontiac's iconic "Styled Steel" wheel with a Pontiac logo in the center, polished stainless trim ring, plus whitewall tires. In one early episode a car can be seen with white-lettered tires, but the whitewalls are more common to the Esprit model, so going forward, whitewalls were used. This is the correct look. *Photo Courtesy Mel Stone*

Three seasons and generations of *Rockford* Firebirds. The 1978 (opposite below) is most unique among them; it is a development of the previous 1974–1975 models. The 1977 introduced the quad rectangular headlight look (opposite above), and the 1978 is very similar, although Pontiac Firebird and *Rockford* aficionados can spot the subtle differences among them. The 1976 (above) still employs a single headlight per side. *Photos Courtesy Mel Stone*

California ROCKFRD

As if three mid-1970s Firebirds aren't enough for one guy, McKinney has a fourth: a 1975 Firebird. It claims no connection to the production of the show, but it sort of looks the part, and so wears this personalized California plate. *Photo Courtesy Mel Stone*

Replicating a Rockbird isn't difficult but requires attention and a bit of research to get the details right. Southern California *Rockford* enthusiast Tom Martin appears to have done just that with this highly authentic looking 1975 *Rockford* Firebird clone. Says Martin, "I started with a low-mileage rust-free Formula 400 and had all the mechanical components of the car rebuilt to factory specs, including the original engine (except for high-compression pistons and a mild cam). The dual snorkel hood was replaced with a standard hood, and the rear spoiler was removed, per the specs for the set-used cars.

"Thanks to some very dedicated people who know every detail about these cars, including Jim Suva and the former stuntman for the show, Roydon Clark, I was able to match the exterior and interior color codes, and other details. It's like I stole one off the set back in 1975; and as fun to drive as if I did."

Pay particular attention to the A75 OKG personalized plate; it's a definite riff on the TV show cars' original California plate. "A 75" obviously stands for the 1975 model year and "OKG" pays homage to the "Oklahoma Garner" reference on the series cars' original blue and yellow stunt plates. Telling the 1975 model from the first season's 1974 car is easy; note the small rectangular driving lights set into the twin front grilles, which you won't see on a 1974. *Photos Courtesy Tom Martin*

AN ENDURING LEGACY *Motorsport Icon*

James Garner didn't race his team's Corvettes, but he drove them on the street and was obviously a 'Vette enthusiast. Here he joins Corvette racer/muscle-car builder/Chevrolet dealer Don Yenko for a victory lap ride-along at War Bonnet Raceway Park in New Mannford, Oklahoma. Garner, a native Oklahoman, was serving as War Bonnet's grand marshal that day. *Photo Courtesy Yenko Collection*

" So, if anybody asks, 'How do you want to be remembered?' I tell them: 'With a smile.'
— *James Garner* "

E ven though his racing days were largely behind him, James Garner maintained his ties to motorsport. He attended races all over the world, particularly world championship Formula One events, and was often a visitor to the Long Beach Grand Prix, the event closest to his Southern California home. He made TV commercials and appeared in advertising spots for Mazda and Oldsmobile. He was inducted into the Off-Road Motorsports Hall of Fame in 1978 for his participation and positive results in off-road racing, and for some of the innovative and unusual machines he drove in the desert competitions.

Chapter Six

Pace Car Memories

Garner also regularly attended the Indianapolis 500 as a VIP guest and visited with his many friends from the racing community. He was asked to drive the Indy 500 pace car on three occasions, pacing the race at the wheel of a Buick Century in 1975 and an Oldsmobile Delta 88 in 1977. For his third and final tour of duty as an Indy pace car pilot, he drove a highly modified Oldsmobile Cutlass Calais in 1985. The combination of James Garner's popularity, celebrity, and considerable prowess behind the wheel of an automobile made him a natural choice for this important assignment.

For many years, a wide variety of individuals had been invited to drive the pace car at Indy, but the process changed considerably after a pit lane crash involving the pace car occurred in 1971. The driver that year was a member of a consortium of Dodge dealers, which provided the pace and parade cars. Indianapolis-area Dodge dealer Eldon Palmer missed his braking point coming out of turn four, and crashed into a photographer's grandstand; several people were injured but fortunately no one was killed. The result, as bad as it was, could have been catastrophic. It wasn't long before the Speedway instituted guidelines about the qualifications and training of the honored pace car driver invitees. James Garner, of course, had no problem

The team that races together eats together, this time with a special guest in the form of James Garner. Garner is seated third from left and Don Yenko is seated to Garner's right, along with the rest of the DX motorsports/Yenko Sportscars, Inc. team and crew. *Photo Courtesy Yenko Collection*

Indy is a world full of smiling, beautiful people. Linda Vaughn (left), the one and only Miss Hurst Golden Shifter and everyone's favorite Motorsport ambassador, with James Garner and "Hurstette" Eloise Colter (right), flash big smiles for the crowd and the camera at the 1972 Indy 500. *Photo Courtesy GM Media Archive*

This is the customized open-roof 1975 Buick Century that James Garner drove to pace the Indy 500 in 1975. His solid performance at the wheel in this role earned him two repeat visits, all aboard GM cars. *Photo Courtesy GM Media Archive*

Garner's second tour of duty as Indy pace car pilot came just two years after his first, this time aboard a 1977 Olds Delta 88, a model not factory-offered as a convertible; this special open-top version was built for the occasion. *Photo Courtesy GM Media Archive*

This Olds Cutlass Calais was an unusual choice for a pace car, but it was a new model in 1985; Oldsmobile was obviously trying to promote it. The prototypical pace car was usually a larger, luxury model or sportier muscle car type of machine with a V-8 engine and rear-wheel drive. This compact Olds was neither; it was a front-wheel-drive 4-cylinder car souped up for more than 200 hp. That was a lot for a small 4-cylinder engine at that time. Regardless, car and driver both performed admirably.

Photo Courtesy GM Media Archive

PACE CAR DRIVER NAMED — Movie and television star James Garner will drive the 1985 Indianapolis 500 pace car, an Oldsmobile Calais coupe. A former off-road racer, Garner starred in the racing movie "Grand Prix" and has recently completed filming "Murphy's Romance" with Sally Field. The pace car, based on the all-new front-drive Oldsmobile Calais, is a specially-constructed open-roof, four-passenger vehicle. The engine, derived from the standard Calais powerplant, is a 2.7-liter, L-4 that produces 215 horsepower at 6,500 RPM.

OLDSMOBILE PUBLIC RELATIONS
LANSING, MICHIGAN 48921

For Release:
Immediately
(April, 1985)

"

You've got 33 drivers with a lot of horsepower behind you, and a responsibility to get off the track.

"

meeting those requirements, and was thus invited three times within a ten-year period to pace the race (high praise and a rare occurrence).

Journalist Lori Lovely has a deep background in motorsport, and interviewed James Garner about his experiences driving Indy 500 pace cars for *Nuvo Newsweekly:* "Driving the pace car is easy and fun," he says casually. "It's not all that difficult. But I'd head for the pits as soon as possible because there were a lot of eager guys behind me!"

Acknowledging the pressure, he says his biggest fear was making a mistake. "You've got 33 drivers with a lot of horsepower behind you, and a responsibility to get off the track." Nevertheless, he also felt a responsibility to the teams and support personnel. Eldon Palmer made a mistake and hit the photographer's stand. "I wanted to avoid that. I never drove fast down the pits; there are too many people there."

About the Indianapolis 500, James Garner said in his autobiography: "I love the traditions and camaraderie of 'the Brickyard.' With 400,000 people cheering and singing 'Back Home in Indiana' it's a unique experience. Even when I wasn't driving the pace car, I tried to go back every year to renew acquaintances and soak up the atmosphere. And whenever

James Garner proved to be the ultimate formula for an Indy 500 pace car driver. He's handsome, popular, and media savvy, not to mention having more-than-adequate driving skills for the job. He commented that the job was easy and fun. *Photo Courtesy GM Media Archive*

James Garner gets into the spirit, and costume, of the early 1900s to help Oldsmobile celebrate its centennial in 1997. The car is one of the late, great, American marque's most seminal and important vehicles: a 1903 "Curved Dash" model. *Photo Courtesy Vista Group*

I was in Indianapolis, I made the pilgrimage to the Iron Skillet for fried chicken and to the Kountry Kitchen for the best chicken-fried steak, mashed potatoes, and gravy in the world."

In 1997, Vista Group Public relations was tasked with putting together several aspects of Oldsmobile's 100th Anniversary celebration, as well as supporting media functions and events. Because of this they ended up having a rare "Curved Dash" Oldsmobile on loan from General Motors. Vista Group's Eric Dahlquist, Sr. and Chuck Koch invited James Garner to visit while the car was at an historic Southern California location called Paramount Ranch (the site of much television and movie filming, particularly westerns, over the years). He accepted the invitation, and arrived decked out in proper early-1900s garb, period appropriate to the car.

Koch notes that "Jim was having a ball, likely as much fun as he's had at the wheel of a car going just a few miles an hour, and not wearing a crash helmet and fire suit." Koch recalls that Oldsmobile used the occasion to commission the filming of a promotional video,

Garner drove the vintage Olds at Paramount Ranch, a historic national park in California that features a full-scale western town used in the filming of many major western movies. The original "Curved Dash" Oldsmobile Model R Runabout, powered by a 95-ci single-cylinder engine, was built from 1901 to 1907, with about 19,000 copies produced. *Photo Courtesy Vista Group*

The Oldsmobile Centennial promotional video that began with James Garner at the tiller of the "Curved Dash" Model R ended with him, in modern formal dress, mugging with Oldsmobile's then-newest model introduction, the mid-size luxury Intrigue. *Photo Courtesy Vista Group*

beginning with Garner at the wheel of the historic 1903 Oldsmobile, and ending with him dressed in black tie, with a then-new Oldsmobile Intrigue.

PJ on JG

James Garner and motorsport legend Parnelli Jones have been friends for more than 45 years. Like Garner, Parnelli Jones has owned and operated his own professional racing teams, and is a member of the Off-Road Motorsports Hall of Fame. Here's what the Indy 500, Baja 500 and 1000, and Trans-Am champion had to say about his actor/racer friend and golfing buddy:

"I first met James Garner in 1968 at the Baja 1000. We were both on Bill Stroppe's Ford Bronco team, and I had gone about 250 miles into the race, and had broken the car. Along comes James and his co-driver Scooter Patrick. I sure didn't want to spend the night, or die, in the middle of the Mexican desert, and we were about 15 miles short of the next checkpoint; we had an airplane that could pick me up at the next stop. So I rode on the back of Jim's Bronco, holding on to the roll bar. I held on so tight, I'm sure my fingerprints are still on that bar. [In *The Garner Files*, James Garner recounts that ride in the roll bar story; it took place in 1970]. That was my first real interaction with him, and we became real good friends after that.

"You have to learn how to drive the conditions. I wasn't a very good off-road racer, even though I won a couple times; I always tended to drive a little too hard for the equipment, but Jim didn't. Thank goodness I had Stroppe around to rein me in a little bit. He finally built me a car that could take my punishment and win the thing. Jim's smart, and he of course knew there was great risk to the other aspects of his life and career in hurting himself, so he learned how to drive the elements; he had a lot on the line. He never drove too far over his head; fast but smart.

"I don't know that he was at a full-fledged pro level; of course he had background doing the open cockpit stuff with *Grand Prix*, and so he did really well. He could hustle the car well without ending up in a ditch. Guys like him and McQueen put a lot of effort into their off-road racing. It wasn't like they just went down there jumped in a car and went for it. They did some of the pre-runs [the off-road racing equivalent of on-track practice] and tried to make the most of it. He did a great job for the limited depth of experience he had. And Scooter helped Jim a lot.

"Jim and I got to be very good friends, and really had a good time when he came back to Indy. You know Jim is an outstanding golfer, and Lloyd Ruby and some of the guys put together some great foursomes. Jim and I hung out a lot in May and played a lot of golf. We played a lot together back here in California too. I've really enjoyed my relationship with him over the years, and still do. He did a lot of good for racing, and did a lot of great driving in his show *The Rockford Files*. I was a big fan of his since the TV show *Maverick*, and so getting to know him was a big thrill for me."

Parnelli Jones is one of America's greatest motorsport treasures, and was one of James Garner's Ford Stroppe Bronco teammates at the Baja/Mexican 1000 in 1968. Garner ran the race in a variety of vehicles over the years, but Jones stuck with Fords, most particularly Broncos, and won the race overall several times. Jones is famously quoted as describing the Baja 1000 as "a 24-hour-long plane crash that never ends." *Photo Courtesy Tom Madigan Archive*

How I Met James Garner

Doug Dwyer started as shop help for Carroll Shelby in 1963, including three years as a tire technician for Shelby's Goodyear Racing Tire Franchise. Dwyer enjoyed a career as sales and marketing manager for Appliance Industries, Eagle One Car Care Products, American Wheels Corp., Weld Wheels, and the Bondurant Driving School; was the general manager of Epsilon Wheels; owner of Simmons Wheels USA and Wheel City LA; and co-founder of Bryson-Dwyer Inc.

He retired as executive vice president of Schiefer Media Inc., and raced motorcycles and road-racing cars, in events that included the LBGP IMSA in 1990, the Daytona 24 Hours, and a Grand-Am podium finish at the Watkins Glen 4-hour in 2002. He ran several off-road races including the Mint and Baja 1000. He enjoyed being a consultant for Shelby, Smokey Yunick, Ivan "Ironman" Stewart, K&N Engineering, Centerforce Clutches, Magnaflow Exhaust, Prolong, Baer Brakes, and others.

He has never worked for a company that was not a SEMA member, except for the U.S. Army, 199th Light Infantry (Vietnam 1969).

The following was originally published in the April 2014 issue of Performance & Hotrod Business *magazine.*

I first met James Garner when I was 16 years old. I was working in Carroll Shelby's Goodyear Racing Tire facility during summers and after school. Carroll Shelby Enterprises was the funding agent of most of Shelby's early projects and Carroll was there often.

I had never really been around Shelby much at that time, so I was surprised when I heard him call my name. "Doug, Jim here needs to get to the airport and I can't take him. I need you to give him a ride, but I don't want you to use your car. Do you think you can take him in his car and get back here without wrecking it?"

James Garner and Shelby were great friends. There I was, standing there with a broom in my hands in front of James Garner and Carroll Shelby. I wish I had a picture of that!

His car turned out to be a Mini Cooper S. We were the West Coast distributor for Minilite wheels and American Racing Equipment; we were going to put tires and wheels on the car. Garner was leaving town and we were going to have the car until he got back.

If I recall it was British Racing Green and it was a blast to drive. I took him to the airport and got the car back without wrecking it. He was a really nice guy. He wanted to know how my life was going and what I was planning to do.

My job at that time was mounting and balancing tires. It was a Saturday morning, relatively early, so I wasn't too dirty yet. (It took me a while to learn how to do that job without getting dirty. It was funny that way, the trick was to work really hard, do a good job, and not look like it. I learned that from a guy named Bud Poorman, but that's another story.)

I think people were really surprised to see James Garner crawl out of that little car at the airport. He was a big guy.

Several weeks later I was working at Riverside Raceway. It was the Times Grand Prix, I think. There were lots of people there for sure. My wife, Jan (my girlfriend at the time), was there with me. All of the tire work was done, so she and I excused ourselves from the garage and started to walk to the snack bar and find a place where we could watch the race.

As we were leaving the garage, Shelby and Garner approached us. Garner had a cup of coffee in his hand and Shelby was selling him something. I said a little prayer that one of them would acknowledge me. They both took notice of us, at least of Jan.

Carroll said hello, and Garner asked me how I was. My heart stopped, and I said a little prayer of thanks. I told them I was fine, then without thinking, I said, "Mr. Garner, this is my girlfriend Jan, she would like your autograph." (I think Jan kicked me, but she now claims she didn't.) Garner graciously reached for her program and handed her his cup of coffee. He produced a pen and signed the program.

I looked at Jan and she was shaking so badly she spilled the coffee. I quickly ran and got him another cup. When I returned, Shelby and Garner were making Jan laugh and having a good time. I stopped for just a second to watch. When I rejoined them, Garner thanked me and they turned to leave. Garner said something to Shelby, and Carroll turned and gave me a little thumbs up.

That moment changed my life forever in ways impossible to imagine. Shelby became a good friend of ours, and we had many great times with him later. The people I met through him, and the things I learned from him, ruined me for the rest of my life!

James Garner is a huge pop-culture star. *The Rockford Files* still has millions of fans worldwide, and there are numerous unofficial websites and forums dedicated to the show; several books have been written about it, too. Toy and die-cast model makers have memorialized several of James Garner's more notable automobiles, including the A.I.R. Lola and 1968 Corvette race cars, as well as the Rockford Firebird (which Mattel's Hot Wheels calls the "Hotbird" on its packaging).

As of this writing, Garner has retired from acting and from all aspects of racing. He still keeps an active hand in his Cherokee Productions Company, living a quiet life in Brentwood, California.

He has proven to be many things to many people; certainly a sort of ultimate car guy to many. He's tall, handsome, and talented on many levels; he's lived his life at a high ethical level. He loves cars, and has had many great ones. He came factory-equipped with a considerable amount of skill as a racing driver, and put that skill to good use on numerous levels; racing competitively at Baja and driving way too fast in all manner of automobiles.

He formed and led a pro-level racing team. He drove Grand Prix cars at speed and in racing situations in an Academy Award–winning film as a headliner. And he burned a lot of rubber in a whole fleet of Pontiac Firebirds.

Not bad for a shy guy from Norman, Oklahoma.

> He came factory-equipped with a considerable amount of skill as a racing driver, and put that skill to good use on numerous levels; racing competitively at Baja and driving way too fast in all manner of automobiles.

Mattel commemorated two of Garner's great cars with these Hot Wheels toys. At left is the A.I.R. L-88 Corvette, wearing a proper race number and team colors. On the right is a loose interpretation of the *Rockford* Firebirds. Curious details include the name "HOT BIRD" with no reference to *The Rockford Files*, and the inclusion of T-top roofs and a Trans Am hood scoop, which the real *Rockford* cars didn't have.

Garner gives a television interview at the Paradise Cove Sand Castle restaurant parking lot in Malibu. The restaurant has since been remodeled and renamed the Paradise Cove Café, and remains a popular visitation spot and photo op for *Rockford* fans. *Photo Courtesy Vista Group*

This is Garner's photo at the Off-Road Motorsports Hall of Fame. He was inducted into this Reno, Nevada, organization in 1978. *Photo Courtesy Off-Road Motorsports Hall of Fame*

INDEX

James Garner has made a distinction between "actors" and "movie stars." There's little question he qualifies as both in the most positive senses. This is Garner's star, in its rightful place on the famous Sunset Boulevard Hollywood Walk of Fame, just outside the main entrance to the world-famous TCL Chinese Theater (formerly Grauman's Chinese Theater and Mann's Chinese Theater) in Hollywood.

James Garner takes a well-deserved bow as a 1994 guest on *The Tonight Show with Jay Leno*, proudly wearing the Pontiac Racing jacket custom made for him by longtime General Motors Racing executive Gary Claudio. Garner appeared on *The Tonight Show* (with hosts Johnny Carson and Jay Leno) many times over the years. *Photo Courtesy Margaret Norton/NBC/NBCU Photo Bank via Getty Images*

Additional books that may interest you...

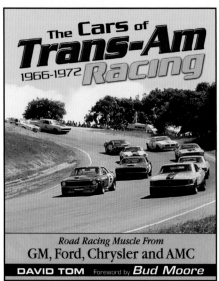

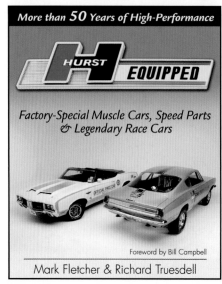

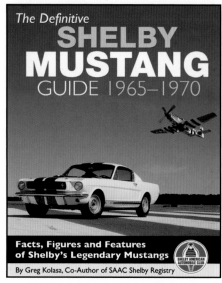

THE CARS OF TRANS-AM RACING: 1966–1972 *by David Tom* When the modified muscle cars of the Trans-Am Series were seen performing well on the country's finest tracks, fans wanted a model of their own in the driveway. These "pony cars" boasted a new look and style not seen before, and their all-around performance eclipsed anything previously accomplished by production-based American GT cars. Author David Tom covers road racing muscle from GM, Ford, Chrysler, and AMC. This book focuses on the cars used in this legendary series. Seeing them in their full competition versions when they were new brings back many fond memories. Hardbound, 8.5 x 11 inches, 192 pages, 500 color photos. *Item # CT516*

HURST EQUIPPED: More Than 50 Years of High-Performance *by Mark Fletcher & Richard Truesdell* No other company or individual had as big an impact on so many aspects of the automotive industry as George Hurst. His performance parts were some of the best ever, the competition cars won many races, and the muscle cars that bear his name were some of the best of the era. Scores of interviews, in-depth research, and exceptional insight from veteran magazine editor Richard Truesdell and co-author Mark Fletcher has created a great book. *Hurst Equipped* captures the complete story from the production cars and race cars to the performance parts. Hardbound, 8.5 x 11 inches, 160 pages, 365 color and b&w photos. *Item # CT490*

THE DEFINITIVE SHELBY MUSTANG GUIDE: 1965-1970 *by Greg Kolasa* Shelby American Auto Club (SAAC) historian and registrar Greg Kolasa details the specifics on the performance and appearance alterations. This book gives a detailed look at both the performance and styling characteristics of each year of the 1965–1970 Shelby Mustangs in text, photographs, and charts/graphs. It clears up many myths and misconceptions surrounding these legendary pony cars. In addition to his firsthand knowledge, Kolasa relies heavily on factory documentation and interviews with Shelby American designers, engineers, stylists, fabricators, and race drivers. Hardbound, 8.5 x 11 inches, 192 pages, 500 color photos. *Item # CT507*

STEVE MAGNANTE'S 1001 MUSCLE CAR FACTS *by Steve Magnante* The author is well known for his encyclopedia-like knowledge of automotive facts. He regularly contributes details on the pages of national magazines and at the popular Barrett-Jackson Auctions on television. The 1001 well-researched facts in this book are the kind of things muscle car fanatics love to know. This book is an informative and entertaining collection of facts from one of the industry's most beloved and respected sources. It covers GM, Ford, Chrysler, and AMC muscle. Softbound, 6x9 inches, 416 pages, 113 b&w photos. *Item # CT517*

Check out our website:

CarTechBooks.com

✓ **Find our newest books before anyone else**

✓ **Get weekly tech tips from our experts**

✓ **Get your ride or project featured on our homepage!**

**Exclusive Promotions and Giveaways on Facebook
Like us to WIN! Facebook.com/CarTechBooks**